OBEDIENCE TRAINING FOR YOUR DOG

BY CECIL WIMHURST

WITH AN INTRODUCTION
BY BLANCHE SAUNDERS

DOVER PUBLICATIONS, INC.
NEW YORK

This book is published in England under the
title "Train Your Dog." This American edition
contains a new introduction by Blanche Saunders
and is for sale only in the United States.

Standard Book Number: 486-20938-5

Manufactured in the United States of America

Dover Publications, Inc.
180 Varick Street
New York, N.Y. 10014

FOREWORD

by

GEORGE SLY

The well known trainer and championship show judge

A VERY famous gun-dog trainer once said to me, ' I always buy any books I see on dog training. There is something to be learnt from them all.' Such modest words from a man who had produced champions shamed me a little, and brought home the secret fact that I personally had sometimes thought myself too great to trouble to study another trainer's methods.

' Something to be learnt.' If that were all, if here and there but a few gems of training lore could be gleaned from the pages we read, Mr. Wimhurst's book would for that reason alone be worth adding to the shelves of a doggy library, containing as it does many useful tips for the experienced trainer. But the author is not one to give himself airs, and has offered his wide knowledge of the subject more as a guide to the beginner and budding enthusiast.

To say, however, that here is a work no novice should miss is to under-rate its magnitude. Rather is it one to start as a novice and to finish as a hard-boiled handler. Everything is here, from the first hesitant moves in obedience to the grand Police Dog Trials finale, and the reader has merely to browse through it and train his dog as he goes along.

Yet I would be rash to forecast unhindered success. The dog is no machine. You do not wind him up to make him go. Neither is he a piece of wood, to be whittled into shape. Nor, as Mr. Wimhurst points out, has he a human brain with which to reason and understand. He cannot talk, but he has actions that speak louder than words, conveying their semaphore meaning. These the trainer must set himself to know.

He has love for his master, an appetite for praise, a sense of fun, virtues that the trainer may use to advantage, or cast aside in folly.

The path of progress bristles and some will lose heart by the way but, to those who persevere, what a reward lies at the end. No words of mine can describe the delights of owning a trained dog. Perhaps it is enough to say that, having possessed one, few would be satisfied with less, for little pleasure can be found in the dog that pursues unheedingly his own particular wants.

Some dogs, it is true, behave well naturally and, without a lesson, yearn to obey. Lucky owners ! No training required here. Still, a glance at the breeding will often show that they have others to thank and not themselves.

Mr. Wimhurst has tackled a difficult task with patience and enthusiasm, backed with his well-known skill with the pen. There are trainers who write—fortunately, here is a writer who trains, flaunting his inimitable style and lively humour in every chapter. I am proud to commend this book to all those who deal with, or are dealt with by, dogs.

HARLENCY,
    MEOPHAM, KENT.

INTRODUCTION
by
BLANCHE SAUNDERS

TWENTY YEARS ago there might have been some excuse for owning a disobedient dog. Today an owner can walk into any bookshop and find a large selection of books on training that will help him teach his pet good manners. With a little more time and the incentive, he can learn how to make his dog a useful, more enjoyable companion, and in so doing, to create an entertaining pastime for himself.

Whether he wants to train his dog entirely at home or whether he enrolls him in a training class, the owner must fully understand and realize his dog's potentialities—which brings me to the point of this introduction.

Every good dog trainer and every person who successfully teaches others how to train their dogs must know psychology, the science which treats of the mind, its powers, functions, and acts. Psychology is more important with four-legged animals than it is with us because animals lack the ability to express their feelings through speech. They must depend upon their more intelligent owners to interpret their thoughts and actions, which frequently puts them at a disadvantage.

I do not know Cecil Wimhurst personally but I have read his book OBEDIENCE TRAINING FOR YOUR DOG with a great deal of interest. I feel convinced that Mr. Wimhurst has made a study of dog psychology. He approaches training in a sensible way. He explains the causes and effects of a dog's behavior so reasonably that it makes the task of training, even for the novice, a simple one.

Dog trainers the world over vary in methods of procedure. I may prefer to use one technique to teach an exercise, while Mr.

Wimhurst suggests another, but basically we try to accomplish the same results. Results are what count. I admire the fact that, even though he may have a different way of doing something, Mr. Wimhurst never loses sight of the most important things in training; namely, patience, kindness, and fair play. I like his style of writing and while reading his book, one gets the impression that he is not only clever with dogs but also with words as well.

Obedience training, though more recently accepted in the United States, is not new to England, where OBEDIENCE TRAINING FOR YOUR DOG was originally published. England has always been known as a "doggie" country and many of our finest specimens of dogdom have England as their birthplace. Even more important, England had the foresight to recognize the value of obedience training for *all* breeds. A trained dog, whether it is a German Shepherd, a Poodle, or a Pekinese, is a happier dog and a more likable companion. It seems fitting and proper that a book on training should have been written by Mr. Wimhurst who has had the experience of a long association with obedience.

Mr. Wimhurst has accomplished a remarkable task in giving us so much information in so few words. The clarity with which the book is written, his knowledge of the subject, and the humorous way he deals with his material, makes me proud to recommend this book to every dog owner who is attempting to train his dog, and especially to those owners whose dogs are attempting to train them.

BLANCHE SAUNDERS
CARILLON KENNELS
BEDFORD, NEW YORK

CONTENTS

Chapter i

MAKING A START

Many owners, fired with enthusiasm at seeing a trained dog work, attempt to train their own dogs but give up after a few lessons fully convinced that the other dogs have that little something which their own dog lacks.

It is true that some breeds are more amenable to training than others, and that individual dogs vary in intelligence, but the chief difference is that the experienced trainer has the know-how while the unskilled novice trains on hit-and-miss methods which tend to confuse rather than teach the dog. All dogs, at any age, can be trained provided the right principles are followed.

All training is based on making use of the animal's natural instincts. The simplest example is in making a dog come at the owner's call or whistle, thus exploiting the instinctive longing of the dog for human companionship. In tracking, the instinct of the dog in searching for food is adapted to the human needs of his handler. The dog, by constant repetition, is taught to perform a certain action until a habit is formed and the word of command is followed by the action.

Training can start when a puppy is a few weeks' old but only the easiest exercises such as sitting on command, habits of cleanliness in the house, and coming when called should be attempted. The latter is important. A puppy who is constantly called to his owner's side and petted almost invariably obeys during later life. Make much of your puppy—pat him, tickle his tummy, and make him feel that there is no fun in life unless he is with you. That way, he seeks your companionship instead of that of other dogs and you will never have the mortification of seeing your dog run off with a horde of canine companions while you shout and whistle in vain for his attention.

But remember that he is a baby and just as much entitled to a carefree life during his early days as any human child. Do not try to teach him too much until he is mature enough to understand. Take it gently and instil in him that confidence and affection in you that will help so much when you are trying to teach him the more advanced exercises.

Regular training can be started at about nine months of age. Opinions differ in this respect and some trainers start earlier or later. Generally speaking, however, a dog at this age is past his first puppyhood and ready for more serious work. Dogs over two years old will need more patience, and the hardest part of the work will be eradicating the habits formed during pre-training days.

It is now that we come up against the age-old question. Which is the easiest to train—a dog or a bitch? There is no positive answer to this. Bitch owners swear by a bitch and dog owners insist that the best results are obtained with a dog. Both sexes have obvious advantages and disadvantages and it is just a matter of personal preference. Incidentally, the use of the masculine gender in this book is to avoid the constant use of the phrase ' he or she ' and in no wise casts any reflection upon the many canine ladies who bear off their fair share of the laurels in the obedience rings all over the world.

The trainer must remember that dogs differ in temperament just as much as humans. There are quick dogs, phlegmatic dogs, clever dogs and those not so clever—there are also dogs who couldn't care less, and these are responsible for many trainers growing old before their time. Get to know your dog and vary the tempo of your training accordingly. Do not hurry the lessons—be sure the pupil has mastered one before passing on to another. He may seem obtuse during the first few lessons but, at last, the blessed moment will come when he realizes that you are trying to teach him something and you will be over the first hurdle and halfway to the second.

So much for the dogs, and now let us consider the more important person of the partnership—the trainer. There are very few bad dogs but there are numbers of bad trainers who blame failures on their dogs when the blame is really faulty teaching. If the lesson has gone awry, the trainer should ask himself if he was impatient, too harsh or too lenient with the dog ; or if he was trying to teach the animal something for which he was not prepared by previous lessons. The chief attributes of a trainer are unlimited patience and the strength to keep his temper when he feels that there is nothing else to do but hit the dog over the head with the sharp end of a pick-axe, bury the body, and take up rabbits instead. We have all felt like that at times and there can be no doubt that our dogs dwell lovingly on the thought of burying their teeth in our shins and calling it a day.

But neither of us do it and we just think that way because only angels have wings—and we're no angels !

So, when you feel impatient and about to lose your temper, pack up the lesson and start all over again at some other time. Go into the house and have a nice cool drink—and presently a cold nose will be thrust into your hand, and he'll sit looking up at you with adoration in his eyes, and you'll wonder what sort of a fiend you are to have even thought that you could ever live without him.

And, very likely, he'll be thinking the same way.

Do not make the mistake of thinking that your dog, however intelligent, has the same thought processes as a human being. No animal can think in the abstract and it is useless to explain to him the purpose of an exercise in the hope that he will understand. Talk to your dog as much as you like. In fact, this will aid training in so far that it will keep his attention fixed on you and the tone of voice will encourage him to try and understand what the lesson is all about.

The tone of voice is important. Commands should be given firmly and distinctly and always use the same command for the same exercise . . . a short word is better than a long word.

Speed is essential in training. Keep the dog moving and follow each command by swift action. Praise and correction must be blended in the correct proportions—and the greatest of these is praise. Your dog should enjoy his lessons, and the more like a game the trainer makes them, the quicker the trainee will respond. The old days when a dog was beaten to make him obey have long since gone and a dog who is seen working in a cowed and dispirited fashion is a living indictment of his owner's incapacity as a trainer.

Correction is carried out by grumbling at the dog in a sharp tone of voice and accompanying this by the appropriate manual manipulation to position him. Most dogs respond to this but there is no cruelty in a quick tap on the nose if the animal is obstinate. No dog resents this, but he will quickly find out if his trainer is weak enough to allow him to get away with wilful mistakes, and bad habits are hard to break. Insist upon the dog obeying before the lesson is finished.

Tid-bits are a help, but do not rely upon them too much. A dog needs an incentive and certain exercises can be speeded if the animal is rewarded with food. It is not good, however, to see a trained dog constantly looking for food after the performance of every exercise. Some animals can only be trained by means of food, but the dog possesses more intelligence than most, and a good dog will be happy and proud to show off his accomplishments without material reward.

It is important to keep to regular periods for training. Fifteen minutes night and morning are better than two hours at a stretch during the weekends. Do not bore the dog. Leave off as soon as his attention wanders badly. A break of a minute or two will work wonders.

Always arrange to take the initial training periods in a quiet garden or park where the pupil will not be distracted. It will be time to take him outside when he has made some progress and it is desired to accustom him to working among other dogs and people.

A harness should not be used for training. Contrary to general belief, a harness is not comfortable to wear. It cumbers a dog's movements and makes him look a sissy. A collar is the correct article and there is nothing like a fine, chain link for comfort. This type of collar has two rings welded on the ends and is so adjusted that it slips over the dog's head, tightening as he pulls against it, and releasing automatically when he ceases to pull. It is sometimes known as a " choke " collar—a quite inaccurate description as it is far less punishing to the neck than a leather collar, which is often badly adjusted, too wide, and much too tight. Chain collars can be obtained in all sizes and can be easily made up for even the tinies.

The leash should be of stout leather and not less than four feet in length. A short lead is useless for training and it pays to start with the right tools. Later on, hoops and jumps will be needed, and mention of these will be made in the appropriate chapters.

Now we are all set to go. We will start with a young puppy

The correct way to hold
a leash — keep it slack

and teach him house manners, skip the next few months of his life while he is growing up, and carry on with a schedule of exercises carefully graded so that each one prepares him for the next.

Persevere and success will be yours. There is no thrill like possessing a working dog who cheerfully obeys your slightest command, and both of you will be respected and envied by other dog owners. Your dog will be happy and you will feel a quiet pride in having trained him yourself. You will have your triumphs and disappointments but the end is sure.

Remember, training a dog is something like learning to ride a bicycle—you think you will never do it, and then, suddenly, you have done it.

CHAPTER 2

HOUSE TRAINING
FIRST STEPS IN OBEDIENCE

A PUPPY has been described as a busy little man who spends his time doing jobs around the house, and the accuracy of this definition will not be disputed by anyone who has attempted to teach a pup habits of cleanliness.

It is not difficult to house train a puppy but it requires patience and unremitting watchfulness for the first week. It should take little more than fourteen days to make the puppy trustworthy—and many are trained in much less than this.

The secret is to watch the pup like a cat eyeing the next door terrier. Snatch him up when he begins to run around in small circles and put him in the garden. Do the same when he runs backwards and forwards with his nose to the ground—he won't be showing an early aptitude for tracking, he'll be a pup with one thought in his mind, and that thought will be detrimental to your dining-room carpet. Get him outside without delay.

Puppies play hard and then flop over and go to sleep. Watch for him to awake and put him outside again. The end of a meal is the signal for another visit to the garden and it is advisable to spend some time with him until you are certain that he is safe to come indoors again.

But mistakes will happen in spite of your vigilance, and there is nothing you can do about it unless you catch the pup in the act. An animal simply does not understand punishment for an action which happened even a few minutes ago and which he has already forgotten. But the time will come when he will misbehave in your presence and you must pick him up, show him his mistake, grumble at him, smack him lightly on the rump, and put him outside. Do not pounce on him roughly or you will frighten him. Pick him up firmly and let the disapproval in your voice be obvious—remember the tone of voice is the thing which counts with a dog. You can call a dog the most shocking things in a kind voice and he'll wag his tail and think he is being complimented.

If this routine is faithfully followed the pup will soon understand that a certain action performed in the house meets with anger, while the same action in the garden is praised, and he'll connect the two sets of circumstances and find the answer. It is a matter of constant watching, never allowing the animal to get away with a wrongful action if he is caught in the act, and always giving him plenty of opportunity to ease himself at frequent intervals.

House training usually breaks down at night when the pup is left to himself. A puppy should not be fed too late and he should have a good run in the garden before being left for the night. However, in spite of this, it is almost impossible to expect him to stay clean throughout the night, while coming down to let him out not only breaks his owner's rest but establishes a bad habit in the puppy and leads him to expect the same attention for the rest of his life. Fortunately, it is a fact that even a very young dog will dislike soiling his bed.

We can make use of this dislike by confining the puppy in a box at night. The box should be large enough to allow him to curl up and stretch in comfort but small enough to discourage strolling about inside. The bottom should be lined with several wads of newspaper and topped with an old blanket which may be thrown away or easily washed.

An old box, obtained for a few cents from any grocer, laid on its side, and with a slatted wood gate, makes an excellent indoor kennel. Smaller-sized boxes may be made for puppies under the size of spaniels.

The dog goes to heel
and awaits the next
command

The puppy should be put inside at night and, for the first night or two, he will very likely object and raise his voice in no uncertain manner. Take no notice, close your ears and ignore him, and he'll soon learn to keep quiet and settle down. In fact, after a few days, he'll recognize the box as his own special domain and resent sleeping anywhere else. It is essential to get the puppy into the open as soon as possible in the morning, but do not make the mistake of opening the door and allowing him to run out. Lift him out of the box and carry him into the garden so that there will be no mistakes on the way to the door. He may wet the box for the first few nights, but this is likely to be the extent of the damage.

House training should be extended to street training. There is no excuse for any owner who allows his dog to soil the footpath, and this disgusting habit is responsible for the periodical complaints seen in most local papers. It is perfectly easy to teach a dog to be clean in the street—just drag him into the gutter when he is about to soil the pavement. Repetition will soon teach him and he will step off the path automatically when he feels the urge.

When the puppy is clean, you can turn your mind to more interesting things and proceed with his education in a simple way compatible with his extreme youth. There is, for instance, the troublesome dog who barks, yaps, screams and whines during the absence of his owners. This leads to trouble with the neighbours and, if accompanied by scratching at the door, damage to property. It is not always convenient to take the dog everywhere and he should be taught that being left is not a punishment but something that will happen as a part of his normal routine.

Puppyhood is the right time for teaching this, and every puppy should, once or twice a day, be shut in a room by himself. He will attempt to follow you, but he should be pushed back gently as the door is closed and he should be told what is happening. Say ' Stay there, good boy, we're going shopping,' or some other phrase, and then leave him. He will whine and squeal at first but you must be firm and on no account give in and go back to comfort him. It may be silly to make a remark to the dog when he cannot possibly understand, but the time will come, as he grows up, when he will understand some words and he will associate the phrase ' going shopping ' with the fact that he is going to be left alone but that you will be back within a short while. In fact, as he grows, the words will be perfectly well understood and he will seek his usual corner upon hearing them without any further delay.

The same procedure is adopted with the car. Accustom him to being left in the vehicle—this can be practised with the car in the drive or garage—and he will soon settle down comfortably to await your return. Incidentally, it is well to accustom a puppy to car riding at an early age. Dogs differ in this respect. Some are never sick after the first trip while others keep it up all their lives. A drink of glucose water before starting may help, or assistance can be sought from a veterinary surgeon, who will prescribe a suitable dose of sedative for the journey. Do not dope the dog unless you are perfectly sure that the tablets will be harmless to him. However, although most puppies are sick during their first ride, this soon passes off and they become hardened road travellers. Do not feed a puppy just before a journey—the food will be wasted within a short while.

The foundations of obedience are laid during early life. Never lose an opportunity of calling the puppy to you and praise him all you know how when he comes. Make him feel that it is a joy to be with you and that coming at your call means that he will be petted and made to feel good. Never scold or smack him if he fails to come immediately—pet him just the same when he makes up his mind to be obedient. A puppy who lags and is then punished when he comes associates the punishment with coming to his owner and not for failing, or being late, in doing so. Morover, it is often because the pup is absorbed in something else and does not hear his owner's call, rather than actual disobedience, which causes the neglect.

There are some puppies which do not respond so well as others. The owner calls, the puppy looks round casually, and then goes on with what he is doing. This is annoying and the owner is inclined to bawl at the pup or try to catch him. Both methods are fatal to success—the one frightens the animal and the other encourages him to run away and make a game of it. It is better to remember that a pup has a quicksilver mind which shifts from one subject to another with great rapidity.

The dog should always
sit in front of the
handler after completion
of any exercise

Make use of this by catching him on the hop. Call him, allow him to disobey, and then wait until he is not looking. Attract his attention by making a sibilant noise with the lips, or hitting him lightly with a thrown fragment of earth, and then, immediately he looks round, call him and make inviting gestures with the hands to call him to you. The pup, taken by surprise, will almost invariably gallop up to investigate all these interesting actions by his owner and the resultant praise will help to reinforce the habits of obedience which are being formed.

And sometimes even that fails, but we have another trick in the bag. We know that chasing him will fail and so we try the opposite—we call him and run away. This will prove an irresistible attraction, the pup will chase you, and you will praise him when he catches up and frisks around your heels. The Golden Rule is to always run away when a dog refuses to come—never try to catch him by chasing. There are other means of making adult dogs obedient but these will be dealt with later.

There is no reason why even a very young puppy should not be taught to sit upon command. This is accomplished by holding the puppy under the chin, pushing his hindquarters into the sitting position, and exclaiming ' Sit ! ' several times in succession. Repeat as necessary. Also, it is a good idea to make him sit before he is given his food dish. Hold the dish out of his reach and order him to sit. Press him down in position if he fails to understand the word. Repeat the procedure once or twice and see that he is in the sitting position, either by his own act or by your placement, before his dish is put on the ground. Puppies learn very quickly this way and their little rears plonk on the floor with an almost frightening thud as soon as they see their dish being filled.

But remember to be gentle with puppies. Their little brains are not yet developed enough to pay attention for long periods. Concentrate on making them so fond of you that their chief delight is being by your side and listening to your voice. Teach them their simple duties and exercises but do it in such a way that they look upon lessons as a game rather than as a penance to be avoided whenever possible.

And now you have made a start. Your puppy is beginning to realize that you are trying to teach him something and his doggy mind will be attentive to grasp your meaning. In a short time he will be old enough to tackle advanced work and we shall be really on our way.

Chapter 3

THE SIT, DOWN, AND STAY

YOUR puppy has learnt to sit on command and he is ready at about nine months of age to start serious training. Each of the following exercises is so graded that each one lays the foundation for the next. Do not hurry—make sure that he fully understands the current lesson before starting on the next.

The secret of successful training largely depends upon the ability of the trainer to keep his dog's attention fixed on him. A dog responds to movement, sensation, and sound. You will have to use all three, plus carefully blended praise and correction, as the more advanced work is taught. Think of training as a triangle laid upon the ground, the three points of which are the sit, the down, and walking to heel. You are going to build a pyramid on these foundations and the apex will be your perfectly trained dog. Be very sure that those three fundamental lessons are well learnt because, without them, it is very sure that the result will be disappointing and even useless.

Teaching an older dog to sit is just as easy as teaching a puppy, and the same procedure is adopted. There is another method which is successfully used, and the trainer should stand in front of the dog, and raise his hands on a level with his chest with palms outwards. Then command ' Sit,' at the same time bending the body towards the dog and pushing the hands forward and downward. The dog will have to raise his head to look at the trainer as he leans forward and will squat automatically. This method has the advantage of making the dog perform the exercise without manual placement by the trainer. It must, of course, be repeated several times before the animal associates the command ' Sit ' with the action.

Is is now time to teach the dog to sit and stay, and this is a test of patience. There is no magic way and only regular

THE SIT   Pressing the dog
into position

lessons will bring success in a reasonable time. Dogs are impatient animals and they hate to be compelled to stay in one place for long. That is why the sit and stay and the long down are marked so highly in obedience competitions. Obedience in this respect is the mark of a well-trained dog and a compliment to the trainer.

Proceed gradually and do not expect the trainee to stay put for more than a few seconds during the first lesson. Sit him and stand in front so that it is easy to push him down if he rises. Command ' Stay ' and let your voice be firm and decisive. Look him straight in the eyes and point a forefinger at him. Act swiftly when he rises—act before he rises if you can—at the least sign of movement upwards, rap out ' Stay ' and dart your finger towards him. If he succeeds in getting up, press him down again quickly. Repeat the command several times and continue repeating it while he sits. If you can get him to stay steady for about a quarter of a minute during the first lesson, praise him and release him.

The next step is to gradually lengthen the time until he is steady for two minutes or longer with you standing right in front of him. By this time you are well on your way and you can now walk slowly round him. He will probably rise and it is then necessary to put him in position again. Repeat the command constantly and do not forget the darting forefinger to reinforce the commands as his head swivels to follow your movements. Most exercises can be taught by means of gestures and voice, and it is well to have a dog who will obey either at the owner's choice.

The time will come when the dog will be steady when you move around him and he must then be taught to stay while you are at a distance and, later on, out of sight. Here again, the secret is to lengthen the distance gradually. Start by retiring about two feet from the dog, using the voice and gesture to bid him to stay. Be ready to go forward quickly and sit him at the least sign of disobedience. Retire a few more feet at each lesson until he will stay when you are something like thirty or forty feet away—longer if you wish. Extend the time in the same way until he will stay for three minutes or more after you have stopped moving.

Do not call the dog towards you when the time is up. Go back to him, stand so that he is on your left side, and make him wait a second or two before he is given the release sign. The recall will come later—concentrate for the moment on making him steady.

It is important to return the dog to his original sitting position if he should get up and creep forward. On no account sit him where he chooses to stop. Drag him back, scold him as you go, and replace him. Also, should he lapse into bad habits after a spell of steadiness and consistently get up when you are at a distance, do not drag him back and then walk back the full distance again. This is wearying for the handler and bad for the dog. Follow the old teaching maxim and return to first principles. Start all over again and stay close to him but, this time, retire to a distance in a shorter time and by longer steps. Some allowance must be made for the age of the dog, and a puppy is naturally more impatient than a mature dog— but only to the extent that the puppy will need more patience and time to make steady. Do not excuse slackness in this exercise and think that he'll get better as he gets older—exactly the reverse will happen and the habit of restlessness will be firmly ingrained and harder still to eradicate.

It is now time to practise steadiness with the owner out of sight. Sit the dog near a hedge, building or some cover in which you can hide and still watch. Retire out of sight and await results. The dog may sit steadily and, in this case, you can thank all the gods you have. The probability is that he will rise almost as soon as he loses sight of you. You must go back to him quickly and start the same weary business all over again—weary, but very worthwhile, as you will discover in later lessons. Sit him, scold him, repeat your command, and hide again. In time, he will know that your absence is temporary and stay until you return.

Much the same procedure is adopted in teaching the dog to lay flat. Start from the sit position, press down with the left hand on his withers, and spread his front legs in front of him with the other hand and arm. Command ' Down ' at the same time and repeat the procedure as necessary. Some dogs learn this quickly and obey, while others understand and will not obey. The reluctant ones can be taught rather more forcibly

THE SIT
Stay close enough to correct
instantly and do not forget
the pointing forefinger as an aid
to enforcing obedience

if, with the dog in a sitting position, the leash is raised in the right hand until it forms a loop with one end attached to the dog's collar and the other end in the trainer's hand. The bottom of the loop should be a few inches above the ground, depending upon the size of the dog.

Command ' Down,' and stamp on the loop of the leash with the left foot and jerk upwards with the hand at the same time. The movement is ' Down foot—up hand ' at the same instant. This will jerk the dog flat. It will not hurt him but he won't like it—it offends his dignity. Also, it increases his respect for his owner, who is obviously not the type to suffer dumb disobedience gladly. Believe it or not, but dogs have a strong social sense and they despise the good-natured chump who allows them to get away with murder.

The above procedure is not easy unless the movement is practised apart from the dog. Its success depends upon a swift, strong movement, cleanly carried through. Fasten the collar around a low, springy tree branch and practise with that. You will become adept after a short while and it is a valuable training weapon which will be useful on many occasions.

The stay at the down differs very little from the same thing at the sit, with the exception that the dog should be trained to remain for far longer periods. Work gradually up to fifteen or twenty minutes, in and out of sight. It is a good plan during the first lesson or two to flat the dog and extend the leash in front of him so that you can step on this quickly and halt any move to sit or rise. If the dog is steady at the sit, there should be little difficulty in training him to stay down.

It is a good plan to flat the dog at unexpected moments. For instance, he should be commanded to lay down while he is playing and the trainer should insist that the command be obeyed without hesitation. Many a dead dog would be alive today if he had been trained to go down promptly upon command instead of running across a road in the path of approaching traffic. It is mistaken kindness for an owner to flinch from the slight inconvenience of inflicting a few jerks on the neck during the training period, and thus subject his dog to the added risk of death on the road through faulty obedience training.

But always remember that praise is more important than

blame. Always end on a successful note and, when your dog
has completed the exercise to your satisfaction, release him and
praise him all you know how.

That way, you'll both be happy.

CHAPTER 4

WALKING TO HEEL

WE have all seen the dog who takes his owner for a walk.
Puffing, panting, straining at the leash, he tows the wretched
human after him and makes a torture of what should be a
pleasant relaxation. The dog who pulls can take all the
pleasure out of ownership and even a small animal will tire a
strong man in a short while.

But the heel lesson, once learnt, remains a habit for always
unless the dog is grossly neglected after training, and the
following method cannot fail to bring results if the instructions
are carefully followed.

Sit the dog by your left side. The leash must be slack—very
slack. On no account hold it close to the neck of the dog.
Command ' Heel ! ' and step off smartly. Most dogs will run
forward and begin to pull and the leash tautens. Extend your
arm, or gain on him a little, so that the leash loosens.
Command ' Heel ! ' loudly and firmly, jerk the leash smartly,
and right about turn. The dog who was in front will now
be behind but he will pass you and start to pull again. Repeat
the process. ' Heel ! Jerk ! About turn ! . . .

Do not be dismayed if the first dozen attempts seem to have
no effect. You will be only making a step or two in each
direction at the first attempts but never let up on the dog. It is
not good enough to allow him to pull for a few yards, repeat
the routine, and then let him pull for a while again. The heel,
jerk, about turn routine must be followed *immediately* the dog
runs ahead. Do everything quickly. Walk fast, rap out the
command, jerk smartly, about turn quickly. If this is done
efficiently the dog should be looking round respectfully when
he hears the command in something like twenty minutes after

THE SIT   Walking round the dog
to teach steadiness
during the sit

the start of the lesson. He will be a very long way from perfect but an idea that he is under discipline will begin to stir in his brain.

A word about the jerk. It is important that the action should be a real jerk as opposed to a pull on the leash. If the dog is pulled he will respond by resisting the pressure and pulling away still harder. The severity of the jerk will depend upon the size and temperament of the animal. A miniature poodle, for instance, will require little more than a twitch on the leash, while a large dog such as an Alsatian or Boxer requires a very definite reminder that his attention is required. Again, a quiet animal, small or large, will respond to a very mild jerk, but a lusty, obstinate type will notice nothing but a strong effort on the part of the trainer.

It is essential to carry out the routine in the command, jerk, about turn order. All training is based on making an animal respond to certain stimuli by word or action. In this case, the ultimate objective is to make the dog respond to the command 'Heel,' and the jerk and about turn are just the means by which he is being taught to recognise the word. Try and see what is happening in his mind during the lesson. He hears the word but it means nothing to him and he takes no notice. He receives a jerk on the neck and then finds that his owner has changed course suddenly and is travelling in the opposite direction. This happens time and time again. It puzzles him and he is kept moving so quickly that he has no time to notice anything else but his trainer's queer behaviour. In a short while he will come to associate the command with the tug on the neck and the about turn of his owner. He will learn that, unless he checks at the word heel, he will feel the jerk. The continuous turning about will baffle him and he will realise that the only way to be certain of his owner's direction is to keep near him.

Some awareness of this should be reached during the first lesson. Every now and again he will be by your side with his nose in line, but not behind, your knee. That is the time to praise him, fondle his ears if he is big enough, and make enticing movements with the fingers to tempt him to stay in position. Talk to him and hold his attention. Pat the side of your knee—plenty of enticing movements will occur to any trainer on the spur of the moment. The main thing is to keep him interested and make him feel that it is a good thing to be walking close to you.

But, when he runs in front again, cut off the praise and the enticing movements like shutting off water with a tap. Rap out a sharp ' Heel !,' jerk the leash, and about turn. Impress upon him that he will not be praised unless he is walking by your side.

The time will come after the first two or three lessons when he will walk with a slack leash and yet not in the correct heel position. He may be a little too far in front or behind. If he is lagging, give a jerk with the leash and entice him to you with the fingers. It is more likely that he will be too much in front and another technique can be used to correct this.

This is the squares and circle method, but it has nothing to do with geometry whatever. It consists of walking the dog to heel round the four sides of a square. Keep the dog on the inside for a start and make all left-handed turns. The drill is quite simple—the dog goes a little way ahead and the trainer should give the command, 'Heel!,' followed a split second later by the turn, in which the trainer pivots smartly on his left foot so that his knee, or part of his leg, catches the dog's muzzle. The animal will soon come to know that the only way in which to avoid the blow on the nose is to keep his muzzle close to the handler's leg so that he can turn with him.

This can be varied by right-hand turns in which the handler gives the command and jerks smartly if the dog does not follow him round or lags. Revert to left-hand turns whenever he tends to go in front too much. Praise as usual when he is in the correct position.

Walking in a left-handed circle is a good way of teaching a dog to keep station. He will be on the inside and the leg and knee of the trainer will be riding him all the time, thus forcing him to keep his nose close to the trainer. The three ways can be combined, interchanged and varied several times during a lesson.

When a fair degree of progress has been made, a dog should be taught to sit squarely by his owner's side at the halt and remain sitting until given the command to proceed at heel. He will have been taught to sit on command and no great difficulty should be found in getting him to sit automatically when the handler stops.

THE SIT   Up right hand, down left!
Teaching a dachshund
to sit at heel when his
owner halts.

Start the lesson and walk him to heel as usual. Halt, command ' Sit !,' raise the leash in the right hand so as to pull up his head, and press his hindquarters down into the sitting position at the same time. Do it quickly and see that he sits squarely. Repeat after a few paces and then again and again. (*See illustration, page* I, *lower right.*) It may take several lessons before he sits automatically at the halt and the command can then be cut out entirely. Insist upon him sitting squarely and close to your leg. Many dogs develop the habit of sitting at an angle with their rears behind the handler's foot. This can be corrected by pushing him into position from behind with the right foot.

Teach heel-work very thoroughly. Practise the dog every day and get him out into the streets and public places as soon as he has reached proficiency. It may well be that he has a relapse upon being taken out into the street for a walk. He may reason that the heel exercise is all very well in the garden or the quiet corner in the park, but pulling is admissible in the street. There is nothing for it but to practise in the quiet streets and gradually work up to the more crowded places. There are deserted streets in every town where turns can be practised and it is well worth while taking great trouble over this phase of your dog's education. There are dogs who work like angels in a competition ring and pull like fiends on the pavements—make sure that your dog is equally at home in the ring and in the street.

But you have not finished yet. He will develop minor faults such as walking wide, and you have yet to teach him to walk and stay at heel while off the leash. Walking wide is not difficult to cure and consists in stepping away, not towards, him, jerking the leash, giving the command, and enticing him close to you by means of your fingers and inviting words. The same routine applies to the dog who lags except that, instead of stepping to the side away from him, the pace should be quickened a trifle.

Do everything quickly. The command, the jerk, and the about turn should follow in quick succession. Walk smartly, turn sharply, keep the dog moving. Praise him when he is in the correct position but correct swiftly when he errs. Never let him get away with an uncorrected fault.

Heel off leash can be attempted when the dog is walking

really well to heel on the lead. Remember, this time you will have no leash with which to reinforce your commands. Your voice is the invisible link between yourself and the dog and it is essential that you keep his attention on you all the time lest boredom overtake him and he breaks away to his newly discovered freedom.

However, if the previous lessons have been well taught, the transition period will be short and the few faults easily corrected. Start him sitting at your side, give the usual command, and move off. Talk to him and keep him interested. He will probably be attracted by a tempting smell and lag behind or go wide. Give the command very sharply to bring him to heel. If he comes, all well and good, but if he disobeys, leash him again and give him several turns on the lead before resuming heel off leash. The same sort of movements and coaxing gestures should be made as in heel on leash. Correct running ahead by the left turns and circle movements. If he runs wild, it is a sign that he has not had sufficient practice on the leash and this should be resumed for a further period.

Training on leash should not be dropped even when the dog is walking well to heel off leash. Give him periods of practice on and off. A dog does not forget his training but he is apt to get careless if the training is not reinforced by frequent practice. Conversely, a dog should not be over-trained. A lesson carried on too long will bore a dog and he will cease to take any interest and refuse to learn. Dogs formed their own ideas about working hours long before the unions came into being and they resent too much overtime.

Try and anticipate the dog's movements when he is walking off leash. His eyes may wander to another dog and it is very certain that a dog's thoughts are straying in the direction of his eyes. Check the budding breakaway with a sharp command to heel and bring his mind back to his work. He may even get the impression that the boss knows everything and decide that further attempts are useless. This is not so far-fetched as it may sound—an owner pouncing suddenly on a dog just as a fault has been, or is about to be, committed does give the animal the impression that nothing he does will be unseen by his master.

However, by now you will have gathered that training a dog to walk to heel is not so simple as it sounds. It needs patience and perseverance but, once accomplished, you have the

Teaching heelwork — the
dog pulls forward

satisfaction of knowing that you have broken the back of the training schedule and that your dog is well on the way to becoming a real companion and a credit to you.

In the next chapter we shall take another step forward but, in the meanwhile . . . Heel! Jerk! About turn!

CHAPTER 5

THE RECALL FROM SIT OR DOWN

Your dog will now sit and flat on command, stay, and walk to heel on and off the leash.

He's come a long way, hasn't he? He is no longer an irresponsible ruffian and has become one of the world's workers. Very likely, he is beginning to look snootily at the other dogs in the street who are ignorant enough to think that heel work means a kick in the ribs.

More important still, he knows that you are trying to teach him something and you are beginning to understand each other.

He should now be taught the recall from the sitting or down position. In this exercise, the dog is left in either position at the discretion of the trainer, who retires twenty or thirty paces away. The dog is called, made to sit in front when he arrives, and then sent round to heel, where he should sit and wait for the next command.

We'll forget about going round to heel for the next lesson or so and concentrate on making him come and sit. This is done by calling the dog and, when he is close to you, rapping out the command ' Sit! ' He may sit at once or halt and look puzzled —probably the latter. In this case, sit him again and retire a few paces only. Call him in and, as he reaches you, catch him up and give the command, pressing him down into the sit position as you do so. Repeat as necessary. It should not be long before he is sitting automatically as he stops, although it may be necessary to give the command several times after the necessity of pushing him into position has vanished.

Do not retire very far until he is competent. In fact, after the first time when a distance of twenty or thirty paces has been chosen for test purposes to see what he will do, it is only necessary to go back a few paces, call him in and sit him, and repeat as many times as necessary. It can, of course, be spread over several lessons. When he is sitting well and consistently the distance can be increased gradually.

Some dogs do not sit close enough to the owner. A sit is good if the dog sits squarely and close enough for the trainer to take an object from his mouth without bending forward unduly— although he will have to stoop for small dogs. If, however, the pupil sits farther away than this, he should be encouraged to come closer by the trainer taking a pace or two backwards, at the same time enticing the dog forward by word and gesture. Fondle his head and pat him when he comes close enough. Insist upon him sitting squarely from the start and gently manipulate him into position by hand or toe if he is at fault. On no account drag the dog roughly forward by his collar— this will make him dislike coming near and undo much of your previous training.

Then teach him to go round to heel at the word of command. There are two methods and both will succeed. Sit the dog, call him to you and have him sitting in front. Wait for a moment and then command ' Heel!,' at the same time pulling him round by the collar until he is at your left side and then making him sit. Repeat as necessary.

The second method is better and swifter, particularly with young dogs who are always naturally hungry. Start with him sitting in front as before and have a piece of meat in the right hand. Show this to the dog but do not let him grab it. Give the command and gradually slide the meat round behind your back, change it to the other hand, and continue the movement. The dog's nose will follow the meat all the way round and he will eventually arrive at your left side. Make him sit and then give him the meat.

Gradually cut out the meat as he begins to obey the command. Feed a tid-bit for the first time, omit it the second, give the third and finish the lesson. Lengthen the intervals in future lessons until he receives nothing at all except praise and an occasional sweetener to keep him happy.

After all, persuasion is always better than brute force.

It should be noted that there is a distinct pause between the handler retiring to a distance, halting, and calling in the dog. There is another pause between him coming in and sitting and being ordered to heel. Some dogs learn the proper sequence of

Heel! Jerk! About Turn!

events but try to jump the gun. In this case, there is nothing else for it but to take the dog back to his former position and make him wait. If he goes round to heel too soon, it will be necessary to restrain him by voice or hold his collar. Whatever the fault, patience will bring the desired result in time.

It is likely that the trainer will run up against trouble after teaching the sit and recall because some dogs tend to confuse this with the sit and stay. This is quite a natural mistake and is usually easily cleared up by correcting the dog and repeating the appropriate word of command very clearly while making the correction. Emphasis is laid again on the supreme importance of choosing a word for an action and sticking to it. Take care over the word and choose something short and sharp. The word ' Hi-hi,' for instance, is much better than the command ' Come.' Repeat them to yourself and see.

Also, it is well to teach a dog to obey a gesture as well as the spoken word. You have been doing this all along by using voice and hands as an enticement. It is now time to standardize your gestures and allot a different one to each exercise. The order ' Down,' for instance, may be accompanied by raising the right hand with the palm outwards and the upper arm in line with the shoulder. The order to heel from the sit in front can be given with a twitch of the finger—appropriate gestures and signs will be easily thought up by any trainer to suit a particular exercise.

But make sure that the dog is following the sign as well as the voice. Interchange voice and signal so that he becomes familiar with both and obeys either. Care must be taken not to blame the dog if he appears to have broken a command. A little thought sometimes proves that a trainer has unwittingly given a signal in conversation with a friend which the dog has picked up and obeyed. This has often happened in the case of the sit and recall and the dog has been unjustly punished for his owner's fault.

The recall may be practised from the sit or down position but beware of allowing the lazy dog to take it from the down too often. It just encourages him to flop on every occasion and he will tend to go down during the sit and stay exercise far too often. It is worth making him sit for the recall even if it means making a few more journeys back and forth to pull him upright and tap him under the chin to make him sit up again.

At this point it will be well to mention that the teaching of a new exercise should not mean that lessons already learnt should be forgotten. The daily training routine should start by allowing the trainee free exercise and then putting him through his routine. Insist upon these being properly performed before the new lesson starts but do not follow a sit and stay with a down and stay. Two periods of inactivity following one another are boring for the dog. Split up a static exercise with a more active one and then follow on.

With the completion of the sit or down recall, your training has taken a big step forward and the way is now open for the retrieve. It is while teaching this that you will appreciate the necessity of well training your dog in the previous exercises.

So on to the next chapter.

CHAPTER 6

THE RETRIEVE

RETRIEVING is one of the most useful accomplishments a dog can possess and it can be one of the hardest, or the easiest, things to teach. It all depends upon the individual dog. Some love picking up an object and returning it, while others regard it as a form of hard labour to be avoided at any cost.

The complete exercise is carried out in the following sequence:

(*a*) The dog sits on the left side of the handler.

(*b*) The handler throws the object and the dog awaits the order to fetch.

(*c*) The handler gives the command.

(*d*) The dog retrieves smartly, sits in front of the handler and presents the object in his mouth.

(*e*) The handler takes the object, pauses, and orders the dog to heel.

(*f*) Dog goes to heel and sits at handler's left side.

It sounds very complicated, doesn't it? But don't despair—we shall break it down and take each part separately. In fact, if you analyse the movements, you will see that your dog has learnt most of them already.

Completion of the about
turn. The dog, which was
in front, is now behind.
Step forward again smartly

You will need an object, and this can take almost any form. Dumb-bells are used in obedience trials for the sake of uniformity and will be found useful for training. Some dog shops stock them; but a length of broomstick cut to a suitable size for the breed of dog, and with a flat piece of wood screwed on either end, will do. If this is impossible, an old stuffed glove, rabbit skin, or something of that nature will serve. Do not use a stick, ball, or any plaything. It will only confuse the dog and he will mix up work and play.

Curiously enough, the initial training is carried out without the object being thrown at all. It is necessary to teach the dog to hold and carry the object before throwing for a retrieve.

This is done by gently opening the dog's mouth and inserting the object. He will immediately drop it unless he is the kind of dog who is too good to live in this weary, wicked world. Pick it up and replace it. Close his mouth and hold your hand under his chin so that he cannot throw it out. Repeat the order ' Carry ' all the time you are doing this. Take your hand slowly from beneath his chin, repeating the command. Replace the object if he drops it—as he probably will. Repeat the sequence until he will hold it for a second. Then take it from his mouth, saying 'Give' as you do so.

Do all this as gently as you can. You must be firm, but avoid bruising the dog's mouth with the object. The lesson will have to be repeated many times before he holds it for a minute or longer, but perseverance will win in the end.

Before going on to the next step we will consider the dog who has learnt to hold the object but refuses to give it up. Two methods may be used to cure this. The first one is to open the dog's mouth with the fingers by taking hold of the top of his muzzle and pressing his lips between his teeth. This is the time-honoured way of opening a dog's mouth but it can be difficult with a strong, determined animal. In fact, it very often degenerates into an undignified struggle ending with the dog as the victor. It is quite useless to strike the dog on the nose in order to make him release—it just makes him more determined and he learns nothing about the art of retrieving in the process.

The second method is to use guile. Hold a piece of meat in front of his nose, command ' Give,' and take out the object as he opens his mouth to take the meat. Out comes the object and in pops the meat and everyone is happy. Use plenty of tid-bits until the habit is formed and he responds to the order to give. Then gradually cut out the bribe—he'll never notice it if it is done carefully.

The next step is to persuade the animal to take the object from your hand. Hold it in front of him, close to his mouth, and command ' Carry.' Tempt him to take it by advancing and withdrawing it. Repeat the command all the time in a coaxing voice. If he picks it up, a distinct advance will be made. If he refuses, repeat the order constantly and place it in his mouth again. Let him hold it for a time, take it away, hold it close to his mouth and try to persuade him to pick it up himself. Keep trying until you succeed. You *will* succeed if you persevere.

When he has got to the stage where he will pick up willingly from your hand, hold the object lower so that he has to bend his head to pick up. He should learn to do this fairly quickly. Then lower it still more, vary the angle at which you present it. Hold your hand level with the ground and, finally, lay the object on the floor and make him pick up from there.

If you are successful, your dog will now pick up an object, hold it in his mouth, and give up willingly. It is now time to teach him to bring it. Sit the dog, make him pick up the object, and leave him. Retire to a distance and then call him. It is the same exercise as the recall from sit or down with the difference that the dog is coming towards you with an object in his mouth. He will come right up to you, sit—and promptly drop the object. For some curious reason, known only to the canine family, a dog seems to think it is impossible to come and sit down while holding a dumb-bell at the same time. It is just one of those things.

He may not even sit because the circumstances are strange for him. He understands the usual recall but the fact of having an object in his mouth makes it all different.

So you teach him once more. If he sits and drops the object, you order him to carry it and pick it up. He may do several things such as standing up to pick it up and then dropping it again as he sits down, or refusing to pick it up at all. The refusal or fault must be followed by immediate action on the part of the trainer, who will place the object in the dog's mouth, hold it there while he commands him to sit if the dog shows

THE RETRIEVE   Teaching the dog to hold
an object in her mouth

signs of refusing to carry, or presses him down into the sit if he stands holding it.

Then there is the dog who brings up the dumb-bell and flings it at the trainer. This shows a happy, independent spirit but it loses marks in an obedience contest and gives onlookers the idea that the dog is doing the training. If the animal persistently drops the object, the trainer must step forward to meet the dog as he comes in, catch him under the chin so that he cannot drop the object, and insist that he hold it steady until taken.

This lesson well learnt, he may now be tested with the thrown object. Sit the dog by your side, show him the object, and throw it. Do not worry about making him wait at this stage. Urge him to fetch it by flicking his ears with the fingers and infusing an excited tone in the voice. The rare dog will retrieve it: sit in front; give it up; and go round to heel on command—the operative word is rare. It is more usual for the trainer to have to knit up the various parts of the exercise in the dog's brain before he gives a perfect performance. However, should it happen, give the dog another throw, praise all you know how if he retrieves correctly, and call it a day. Do not weary the pupil by needless repetition. End on a successful note.

If the dog goes after the dumb-bell but just sniffs at it without making any attempt to pick up, do not scold or blame him. Think it out for yourself—you are several yards away and all the shouting in the world will not make a dog pick up if he is determined not to do it. You are too far away to place it in his mouth and, if you go up to him and do so, the whole object of the lesson has been lost and the animal still has not picked up at a distance.

The correct procedure is to make a game of it. In all probability the dog is not being wilfully disobedient—he is just puzzled and uncertain. Call ' Fetch it, good boy,' and run away from him. Incite him by word and gesture to pick it up and bring it to you. Return to the object, pick it up, throw it a short way, play with it, arouse his curiosity, and sooner or later he will pick it up and bring it to you. Lavish praise upon him when he does this and forget about all the other parts of the exercise such as sitting in front and going to heel. Concentrate on getting him to bring the object to you and, when he is doing this as a matter of routine, and retrieving from your side, make him sit in front. It is easy to teach him to wait before running out on the retrieve by holding him back by the collar until the command to fetch is given. He will soon learn to await the word of command and it should be noted that the best retrievers are often impatient and keen. A retrieve should be quick and workmanlike—the type of dog who creeps back to his owner with belly low to ground is not the sort to emulate.

A dog who has been properly trained by this method rarely gives much trouble and ends up as a reliable retriever. There is, however, a type of dog who is resistant to the method advised in the previous pages. This kind of dog is usually very impatient and active and acts like a fish on the end of a line if any attempt is made to hold an object in his mouth. The unfortunate trainer struggles to insert a dumb-bell between jaws which are never twice in the same place. It becomes a trial of brute force.

In fact, the trainer is likely to end up by finding he is holding the object in his own mouth—which makes the trainer look a fool and leads to the dog sitting back on his haunches and laughing his head off.

But do not despair. The dog will still make a good retriever, but he must be taught the play-way. Forget all about placing anything in his mouth and making him hold it. Throw the object and incite him to fetch it. Act as you would with a dog who has been taught by the first method but who will not pick up the thrown object. Throw the dumb-bell a short way, run away from him, pick up the object yourself and toss it about. In short, do all you can to arouse the dog's sense of fun and curiosity. Praise lavishly at the least sign of a retrieve and call it a day when he has made one successful pick up. Be sure that he will retrieve regularly before passing on to the finishing touches such as the sit to present and the return to heel.

A dog should never be hit or scolded severely while being taught to retrieve. One hasty tap on the nose can destroy the patient work of days—it can even finish any chance of teaching the pupil to make a really good retriever. A sad shake of the head and a weary tut-tut is just about all that should be given —and after that, it is usually better to end the lesson and try again when trainer and dog are both in a better mood.

THE RETRIEVE   The dog must be
encouraged to hold
the object steadily.
Note the pointing
forefinger

Remember, no machinery exists to make a dog pick up an object if he refuses to do so while at a distance from his trainer. He can be persuaded but never forced. One more thing can be tried and this is often successful. Let the trainer tell the dog in a bored voice that he doesn't care if he never picks up the darned dumb-bell, and then walk away in a bored fashion. More than once, a disobedient dog, out of sheer pique, has picked up the object and run after the trainer to present it to him.

The complete retrieve, except for the rare natural retriever, is a difficult thing to teach but it must be learnt if the dog is to go on to tracking, scent discrimination, and the seek-back and forward. A lot of patient repetition will be required before the dog performs the whole sequence smartly and correctly. Do not be discouraged if the task seems endless. After all, you have progressed so far, your dog has learnt all the previous exercises, and he is just as anxious to learn as you are to teach. It is a fact that dogs are worried until they have learnt to perform an exercise well. They hate to be puzzled in their minds and even the wayward ones show signs of pride when, at last, they earn the praise of their owner and know that they have mastered their task.

So don't give up. The blessed day will dawn when everything will fall into place and the dog will behave like an angel —maybe you will even see the ghosts of those obedience test cups glimmering on the sideboard!

Just keep trying and they will be there in reality.

CHAPTER 7

SCENT DISCRIMINATION—THE SEEK-BACK

THE dog who is able to distinguish an article bearing a certain scent from others in close proximity carrying a different scent, and bring the object back to his owner, will be found useful upon all sorts of occasions. This exercise, taught in conjunction with the seek-back, will enable the trainer to send him back to fetch a forgotten article, or seek out something which has been lost.

It is essential that the dog should be taught how to discriminate scent if he is to be used for this work. It is quite useless to tell him that he is to search for a lady's handbag, made of brown leather with a gilt clasp, and shaped like a hexagon. If he is given the scent of the owner of the handbag, the well-trained dog will understand perfectly well and bring back only an article bearing that scent.

It will be seen, therefore, that the seek-back and the scent discrimination exercise are really extensions of the retrieve with the difference that the article is not thrown and that the dog has to seek it out before retrieving it.

Use an article of your own for the first attempt. Anything will do—a glove, a wallet, or even a clothes peg or an empty cigarette packet. Place this on the ground and then have an assistant place various other objects near it in any pattern or order.

Do this with the dog sitting a few paces away and in full sight of the procedure. Go back to him, place your hand over his nose in order to give him the scent, saying ' seek . . . seek . . . seek.' Take your hand away, gesture towards the objects, and tell him to fetch. More often than not he will go straight to the line, sniff along it, and pick out the correct article. Call him to you, make him sit and present as in an ordinary retrieve, and send him round to heel. Do not forget to praise him.

Some dogs play with the first object they find while others, confusing it with the retrieve, bring back the wrong article. Whatever the mistake, do not correct harshly or you may have difficulty in making the dog go at all. Take the faulty item away and send him again. If he fails the second time, walk down the line by his side, pick up the correct article, let him smell it, and encourage him to pick it up. Praise him when he does so and then repeat the exercise from a distance again. Repeat as necessary.

Make sure that your hand does not touch any other article than your own when doing this. The slightest touch will scent the object and a keen-nosed dog will pick this up. If your article is placed in position by an assistant, it should be placed on a flat newspaper, tray, or any convenient receptacle and dropped from that among the others. A dog can, and will, analyse the various scents on anything, but there is no point in making it difficult for him during the first lesson.

THE RETRIEVE   The dog now holds
the object steadily.
despite interruptions
and movements near her

This is not usually a difficult exercise to teach. The dog who is lacking in scenting ability is very rare and failure is usually caused by lack of interest on the part of the dog or pure obstinacy. Very few dogs fail to pick up the skill and many come to it almost without being taught at all. It is an ideal exercise to teach in the house and it will help to play hide and seek with the dog. Sit him in the room and let him see you hide something. Send him after it and praise him when he finds it. Extend the game to hiding the article in another room, making it more difficult each time. He'll love the game and it will help to instil a tracking sense into his brain. Do not forget to give him the scent before sending him to search. This is important. He must be taught to expect a scent clue before he is sent to find anything.

The next step is to have him fetch back an article bearing a strange scent. Have as an assistant someone he knows and place the assistant's article among articles not bearing your own scent. An object of your own will only confuse the dog at first.

Then ask the assistant to place his hand around the dog's nose so that he may get the scent. Keep the hand long enough in position for him to drink in the new scent. Send him to seek-fetch.

He may pick up the article at the first attempt but the probability is that he will search around, lift his head, and look puzzled because of the absence of anything bearing your own familar scent. Encourage him to seek-fetch for a few moments. If he still seems uncertain, call him in and give him the scent again. If this is unsuccessful, call him in, give him the scent, and go down the line with him, encouraging him as he sniffs at the correct article. Encourage him to pick it up and present it if he hesitates at retrieving it. Repeat as often as necessary.

When the dog is discriminating freely on your own and a stranger's scent, test him frequently with different people. Also, it is a good plan to vary the scent taking by making him take the track from a footmark on the ground. Start with your own, change to a stranger's mark, and give the dog the scent by sitting him a few paces away, pointing to the mark and calling him in to examine it with his nose. Coax him to sniff but be careful that you do not touch a strange mark in any way or the scent will be fouled. The idea of sitting the dog a few paces away is to arouse his curiosity as he watches you examining the ground. He will be eager to smell the interesting patch when he is called up and thus take the scent thoroughly.

The seek-back is a variation of the scent discrimination test and it is also a simple form of tracking. As usual, make the early stages as simple as possible.

Hold the object in the right hand and walk with the dog at heel. Proceed about ten paces and drop the article, walk another ten paces, halt, give the dog the scent with your hand, wave in the direction of the article, and command him to ' Seek-fetch.' Encourage him to go back. He is certain to see the object at such close range and should retrieve it easily. Praise him when he brings it back, call him to heel, and proceed with the walk.

The next phase is to increase the distance. Walk thirty yards and then send him back. Increase gradually but keep to a straight line. Do not worry about the article being out of sight. The dog will retrieve by sight so long as he can see the object but, provided he knows that he is being sent back to retrieve it, he will naturally drop his nose to the ground and track back by scent. As the distance becomes longer he may tend to become disheartened and give up halfway. He must be encouraged to keep going—even if this means walking a few paces behind him and encouraging him to seek all the time. Never find the object yourself and show it to the dog. Encourage him to find it—even if you are almost standing on top of it. Sooner or later, he'll pounce on it and rush up to you with his tail wagging, quite certain that he has done all the work and that he has accomplished a wonderful and breath-taking task all on his own. As a wise owner, you will praise him and let him take the credit. A dog, once helped by his owner, tends to look to him for help and loses initiative. Moreover, finishing the seek-back teaches him that there is always something even at the end of the longest trail and he learns to keep going.

Also, do not call him when he appears to be following a different line to the path travelled before he was sent back. This is due to the scent being carried by a cross wind or a similar reason. More will be said about this when we come to tracking.

**THE COMPLETE
RETRIEVE**

The handler throws and
the dog waits until
commanded to fetch

THE COMPLETE RETRIEVE

The dog goes forward and returns with the object

When he is seeking back successfully on a straight line, turns to right and left may be introduced. Drop the article, walk on, and a few paces farther on, turn to right or left, proceed another few paces, halt, and send him back. The dog may shoot off and over-run the line but he usually realises that there is a lack of scent, drops his nose to the ground, and begins to search. Let him alone as long as he is working but guide him unobtrusively when you are sure that he is well off the track and losing heart.

This is mainly a matter of practice and more turns can be introduced as the dog becomes proficient. Test him frequently and give him the opportunity to show his skill by sending him back long distances when out for a walk in the woods or fields. It is not necessary to keep a trained dog to heel all the time—he can be called in, given the scent, and sent back to retrieve the article whatever he is doing at the time. In fact, it helps to teach him real work as opposed to a training period and he learns to work apart from a regular routine.

The majority of dogs become very keen on both exercises—in many cases it is difficult to make the dog wait for the command before setting off on a scent discrimination or a seek-back. The latter is one of the most useful exercises taught. Most of us drop something at one time or the other but why go back for it? Send the dog instead.

After all, we have only two legs and he has four—plus a nose to discover anything which may lay concealed.

So let him work for his living—he'll enjoy it.

CHAPTER 8

THE SEND-AWAY, DROP, AND RECALL

THE object of the Send-away exercise is to train the dog to go in any direction at the command and gesture of the owner. This is necessary because the dog may have to quarter the ground in a given direction to find a lost article; while shooting; or to locate a suspected intruder in police and guard work.

The exercise is divided into three parts:

(a) The dog is sent in the required direction.

(b) He is dropped flat when he has gone far enough, This is taught because the dog may be running into danger if he proceeds or the owner may want to shoot over him. There are many reasons—all easy to imagine.

(c) The dog is taught to stay in that position, no matter what the owner's movements, until recalled to heel.

This exercise is not easy to teach because of the natural dislike of the dog to being sent away from his master and he finds it difficult to understand why this should happen. There are various ways of teaching it but the best method is the one evolved by Mr. George Sly, Meopham, Kent, who has kindly given permission for it to be quoted in this book.

Fasten a stake firmly in the ground—a garden fork will do—and attach a long rope to the dog's collar, passing the other end round the stake. Stand about ten feet away with the dog on your left side and holding the end of the rope in your hand. Have a tid-bit ready.

Gesture sharply towards the stake with the right hand and command ' Away!,' and the dog will advance a few steps or stand still in astonishment. Whichever he does, the next action is the same. Pull gently on the rope and so pull the dog round the stake and back to you. Make a fuss of him as he comes back and give him the reward. Repeat until he runs freely around the stake at the gesture and command ' Away!,' and gradually increase the distance to about twenty feet on the rope. By that time, he should be going round off leash but should be re-attached to the rope if he shows signs of uncertainty at any time. Forget all about dropping him for the time being.

This accomplishes the first part of the training but, so far, you have only taught him to run around that stake and he is under the impression that this is the sole object of the training. Keep him thinking this and do not forget the tid-bit every time he returns to you. The next step is to get distance, and this is obtained by planting a stick at ever increasing distances until about a hundred yards is reached. You may choose any distance to suit yourself but see that it errs on the long side rather than the short.

As the distance increases, the dog may hesitate, run a short distance forward, or even refuse to go at all. When this happens, take him by the collar, lead him round the post, and back to the starting point. Repeat the command as you pull him forward. Send him again. If he still fails, shorten the distance a little, lead him round, and send again. Lengthen the distance for the next attempt. It may be necessary to do this several times.

The stick can be varied by using other marks such as a clump of grass, a sapling, or even a bicycle. Get him used to running around any object indicated to him at a distance. Always lead him around if he appears to be puzzled or refuses.

The time has now come to teach him direction. Close up the practice distance a few yards and plant a stake. Then plant another one at an angle of ninety degrees, standing with the dog at the angle thus formed, an imaginary line forming the arms running from trainer and dog to the stakes. These should be an equal distance apart.

Then send the dog around one of the stakes, praise and reward as usual when he returns, and then send him round the other. Be sure to make the gesture very clearly. Call him back if he makes a mistake and goes towards the wrong stake. Send him again. If the mistake is persistent, you must lead him round the correct stake and send him around both alternately until he obeys correctly.

The time will come when your dog will feel quite sure that he is going to find a stake or other object as a turning point even if he cannot see it. You will use this delusion to wean him from always making an object the point of return.

Do it this way. Plant a stake and send him round it. Then send him in another direction. He has been used to finding a stake there, too, and he will feel confident that he will catch up with it if he keeps going long enough.

Only this time there is not a stake at all and the trainer must allow the dog to go away a sufficient distance and then call him back. This leaves the dog's faith in the invisible post undisturbed and he thinks he is leaving the job half finished at the command of his owner. The next step is to remove the other post and practise sending the dog in various directions. If the dog falls off in performance, or becomes puzzled, return to the post for a lesson or two.

Do not on any account drop the dog at this stage. Keep him

on his feet and call him back when he has gone a reasonable distance. It is not necessary to send him towards an invisible object all the time. Vary the routine by sending him round anything you like so long as it is some distance away. Mix sending him into the ' blue ' with sending him round as many varied objects as you can think up. The main thing is to get him accustomed to going away from his owner on command and in the direction required.

The drop can be introduced at any time now and it is important that the dog, once dropped, shall not run to his owner even if he is moving away. The dog must be perfectly still until recalled to heel by command or gesture. There are several reasons for this. The owner may be hunting and wish to take a shot from a different angle, or, in police work, it is sometimes necessary to leave a dog watching while the police-man investigates in another direction. There are many easily imagined reasons besides these.

It should not be difficult to get the dog to drop. He has been taught this and thoroughly understands the command. He may hesitate because this particular command has never been associated with the send-away before, but a sharp repeat command should ensure obedience if the preliminary training has been carefully carried out.

So drop the dog and walk across his front for about twenty or thirty paces, turn towards him and walk right up to him, turning about as you reach him and walking away. He may get up and follow. Drag him back to the original spot, scold him sternly and make him stay. Walk away from him again and repeat the performance until he is perfectly steady and makes no attempt to run in to heel as you about turn and walk away from him. Vary this by walking behind and around him. When he is steady, practise calling him to heel from various distances and angles.

At this stage, a snag will rear its ugly head. The dog will come to believe that the object of the exercise is to send him away and that the drop is the all-important thing. He will tend to go for a short distance, look round, and await the command to drop. He may even drop automatically when he considers he has gone far enough away.

So long as the exercise is unrelated to practical work, one cannot blame him for thinking this. After all, according to his

**THE COMPLETE
RETRIEVE**

The dog presents at
the sit, waits until
handler takes the object

**THE COMPLETE
RETRIEVE**

The handler takes the object
and the dog is ordered
to return to heel

reasoning, he is sent away from his master just to drop at a distance—a simple exercise which could very well be performed at his side. Nothing except the recall to heel follows the drop and an intelligent dog feels frustrated and regards the whole exercise as a queer foible on the part of the trainer which must be humoured. In practical work, such as in shooting, where the dog is sent forward to flush game and dropped before the shot, he soon associates the sequence of events and the actual drop becomes just part of the operation.

Everyone, however, has neither the wish nor the opportunity to indulge in shooting or practical police work, and the send-away to them is an obedience test only. It is necessary in this case to avoid dropping the dog every time the exercise is practised. By all means send him away, around obstacles or into the ' blue,' praising him as he returns or is called back. Leave the drop until it is really required as a demonstration or in the obedience ring. Do not be afraid that he will forget this part of the exercise. In any case, a speedy drop should be regularly practised by flatting the dog at unexpected moments such as when he is playing or out for a walk.

The Send-away is not an easy thing to teach but it is a proof that the trainer knows his job and that the dog has plenty of working ability. It is part of the Kennel Club schedule of working trials and obedience tests, and entry in these will prove interesting as well as being a means of measuring the capacity of one dog against others.

Keep going. We have broken the back of the job and the end is in sight. A little more effort and your dog will graduate as a fully trained working dog.

You'll be proud of him.

CHAPTER 9

STANDING ON COMMAND
THE ADVANCED SIT, STAND, AND DOWN

TEACHING a dog to rise and stand from a sitting or down position is very much the same as training him to sit or go down. It is easier to start from the sitting position.

Sit the dog in front of you, hold his collar, command him
' Stand,' at the same time pulling him slightly forward by the
collar and pushing gently upwards with the toe of the right
shoe under the belly. Repeat the command continually while
this is taking place. Hold him in position for a few seconds,
repeating the command all the time, and then sit him again.
Repeat the procedure half a dozen times in succession and
then try the command alone. Go back to the command and
manual placement again if he does not understand. Repeat
as necessary.

There is another way. The command is repeated continually as above but the trainer bends over the animal with
one hand on his collar and the other under the belly of the
dog. The only difference is that the hand raises the dog into
the standing position instead of the toe of the shoe.

There is no other way of teaching this except by patient
repetition. It is sit . . . stand . . . sit . . . stand . . . sit . . . stand
. . . until the dog obeys on command alone. It is not difficult
to teach and can be introduced anywhere in the training
schedule. Make him stand from the down position when he
has learnt to stand from the sit and understands the command.
Also, it is advisable to teach him to stay at the stand for at
least a minute. This is done in exactly the same way as the
down and stay and the sit and stay. The trainer stays close
to the dog for the first two or three lessons and checks instantly
any attempt to move, sit, or go down. Remember the rule—
instant correction is twice as effective as correction delayed
until the trainer covers a distance and reaches the dog.

Stick close until the trainee understands what is required
of him and correct like lightning . . . always. Remember
the darting forefinger and try to anticipate the act of
disobedience.

When he can sit, flat, and stand upon command, the
advanced sit, stand, and down, may be taught. In this
exercise, the trainer walks with the dog at heel, commands
him to sit, stand, or flat, while on the move, and walks on
without a pause, leaving the dog in the required position. The
trainer continues to walk around the ring until he reaches
the dog again, commands him to heel, and they both continue
the walk together. The exercise is completed by giving the
dog the remaining two commands.

THE SIT   Remote control by signal

THE DOWN   Remote control by
signal

Your dog has already learnt the essentials of the exercises and the only new parts about it are the command to sit while both owner and dog are moving, and the pick-up to heel and the continuation of the walk as the trainer comes back.

Start with the sit. Walk briskly with the dog off leash, command ' Sit!,' at the same time pushing the flat of the left hand back in a retarding gesture. You will have to slow a little to do this and it is probable that he will halt, look undecided, and follow you. Glance round and come back to him immediately, take him back to the original position, tell him to stay, and walk on. Return as many times as necessary but always complete the circuit before picking him up to heel. It is realised that it will not be possible very often to continue walking after the command is given because the dog almost invariably hesitates and follows during the first few lessons. Make a habit of glancing back during the first one or two paces after the command and, if the dog has disobeyed, swing round on him, give the order in a very firm voice, and press him into position swiftly if this is necessary.

It is helpful sometimes in the early stages if, when the command is given, you swing round as you give the command, and walk a few paces backward so that you face the dog, while repeating the command by voice and gesture to stay in the required position. The main thing is to make him understand that he must instantly assume the position and stay even if his owner continues to move away from him.

Practise with one position first. The sit is generally convenient and well known by the dog. When he has learnt this, teach him another position and then the third. Then mix them up and change the order about until he obeys instantly whatever the command. Later on, it will not be necessary to look round at all. In fact, once the dog is well trained, it is harmful to do this as the animal may mistake the glance as an order to come to heel. Also, when picking up the dog at heel, it helps to accelerate the pace a little as you come close to him, and give the command ' Heel! ' a fraction of a second before you draw level. This gives the dog time to rise and the faster pace ensures that he steps off with you at the correct heel position without lagging.

The exercise can be applied practically in the street for many reasons. You may, for instance, wish to cross the road and find that it has been freshly tarred. The tar will not injure your shoes but a dog with tarry paws is apt to have his feelings hurt when he realises that everyone shrinks from him in horror when he makes affectionate advances!

So leave him in one of the stay positions while you pop across to glance in the window of the little shop across the road, come back, and pick him up at heel as you move on.

This is quite an advanced exercise and your dog should now be accustomed to dropping into any of the three positions as soon as commanded. It is now time to consider the dog who, although otherwise trainable and obedient, has the irritating habit of running off to play and refusing to come to his owner when called.

This is a difficult problem to solve and much patience is needed. It will make matters worse if the dog is punished when he eventually makes up his mind to return and, whatever the state of the trainer's feelings, the animal should be praised as he comes up. He must be made to feel that it is good to be by your side, so praise lavishly—even if you feel like giving him away to the nearest junk man in return for a cigar or a coconut!

One way of teaching him obedience in this respect is to put him on a long line and let him wander at will. Do nothing until he begins to run away and then call him. He will take no notice so continue calling, hold the rope firmly, and let him run on until he is brought up with a jerk. Call him to you, pulling on the rope if he is reluctant, and then praise him when he is in front of you. It is a slow process and may have to be continued for days—or even weeks.

Another method may be tried if your dog has been thoroughly practised in flatting on command. If the training has been right, the animal will go down instinctively as soon as the order is rapped out. Take advantage of this by flatting him directly he starts to run off and follow this by a swift command to stay. Keep him down for a few seconds, move a short distance away, and then call him. Praise him when he responds.

It is really a question of replacing a bad habit with a good one. Constant flatting as soon as he shows signs of going away does two things to his mind. It reinforces his obedience training and grooves instant obedience to the command deeper

THE STAND   Remote control by
             signal

**ADVANCED
TRAINING CLASS**   The long sit with
owners out of sight

into his mind, while the call up to his owner, and subsequent praise, makes him feel that it is pleasant to respond.

But your actions will have to be quick and the command must follow instantly when the dog is seen to make a move. Watch his eyes—a dog thinks where he is looking and it is often possible to forestall temptation and anticipate the dog's action. Both methods may be used in conjunction with each other.

Be patient, train at regular intervals, and you will succeed sooner than you think.

CHAPTER 10

REMOTE CONTROL
JUMPING THROUGH A HOOP

THE remote control exercise is not difficult for the dog who is well on with his training. Competitive obedience tests require that he obey the commands sit, down, and stand, mixed up in any order of six commands, the dog not to pass over a line placed six feet in front of him.

It is a good idea to make the distance five feet. It will accustom him to working in the more restricted area and he will be more likely to succeed at the real competitive distance when necessary.

The dog has already been taught to sit, stand, and flat while stationary and on the move. The chief trouble will be in getting him to obey his trainer while at a distance and yet stay within the working limits.

The first problem is easily solved by giving the commands while close to the dog and gradually moving to a distance. The dog may not obey at all at the first command. Do not think he is stupid because he has obeyed the same order hundreds of times before. Dogs are creatures of habit and dislike change. He will not be stupid—just puzzled because he senses that this is something different. Be patient and correct him at once and then repeat the command.

Most dogs come over the line at first. This is another reason for standing close to him. Push him back when he comes over the line and repeat the routine. This is sufficient for some dogs but others are not cured of the habit so easily.

In this case, fasten the animal to a post with the leash just long enough to limit his movements forward but not so short as to prevent him sitting, going down, or standing, in comfort. Give the commands repeatedly while he is tied and then try him free. See that he does not become entangled with the leash or he will worry about this instead of paying attention to the orders.

Another effective method is to place him on a table or bench so that he cannot come very far forward without falling over the edge. This is a very effective method although he may jump to the ground when he reaches the limit. Cure this by scolding him and replacing him on the table. Insist upon him obeying the commands just as if he was on the ground. Do not continue with the table once he has learnt to obey all the commands without moving very much at all. Transfer him to the ground or he may get into the habit of thinking that a table is essential—and, while there is no absolute rule about bringing your own table to an obedience show, some of the less humorous judges may think it eccentric on your part and insist that the exercise is performed on the ground.

Dogs vary a lot while performing this exercise. Some can assume the three movements and hardly move an inch either way, while others seem to need the entire limit of six feet. Also, there are dogs who fully realize the meaning of the line in front of them and insist on coming right up to it although they rarely overstep. In fact, a dog has been known to be hard up against it at the fifth command, which was to sit. The next position was the down and the dog realized that he would have to cross the line if he obeyed. He looked at his owner and then deliberately turned his body parallel to the line and lay down within it.

And some people say that dogs cannot think!

Use the darting forefinger freely to check any command to come forward. Snap out the command and the finger together. It will have a most deterrent effect on the dog. Also, if a dog is reluctant to assume the stand position, he may be given the order in a ' calling ' voice. This will give him the momentary impression that he is being recalled and he will rise—only to be checked by the forefinger. It is only fair to say, however, that this is a doubtful method as it tends to confuse the dog and it

**ADVANCED
TRAINING CLASS** The long down with
owners out of sight

**ADVANCED
TRAINING CLASS**   Practising the advanced
sit, stand and down

is not always easy to check the first step or two forward. Use it only as a last resort.

The sense of teaching this exercise is sometimes queried, but its use is obvious and it has saved the life of more than one dog. You may be on the other side of the road and your dog is about to bound across to you in front of fast-moving traffic. The trained dog will obey your order to stay immediately and go down on the spot, but the unfortunate untrained animal will want to get to his owner first . . . and there is another pathetic bundle of bloodstained hair on the highway.

And now we'll take a little time out from the more serious side of training and teach the dog to jump through a hoop. Everyone likes to see this and it is one of the oldest animal tricks in the world—and one of the easiest to teach.

Buy or make a hoop large enough for your dog to get through easily. Hold it just an inch or two above the ground and put your dog on one side of it and hold a piece of meat on the other.

Command ' Through! ' If he goes round the hoop, push him back and repeat the sequence. Refuse to give him the meat until he hops or walks through. Repeat for a time or two and raise the hoop another few inches. Repeat continually until he is jumping well with the hoop well above the ground at a height consistent with the size of the dog. When he is proficient, reduce the size of the hoop until he will jump through something quite small. The meat can be withdrawn after a while. Make a game of it and he will not mind this. As the height of the jump becomes greater it will be necessary to sit him at a distance and make him wait until commanded to jump.

You may make him burst through a hoop covered with thin paper if you wish. Start with the paper just fringing the circumference of the hoop and leave plenty of room for him to get through. Increase the area of the paper gradually, leaving a smaller hole in the middle each time, until, finally, the hoop is covered entirely. Use easily tearable paper until he becomes used to it. Tissue paper is ideal and is not too opaque.

People do this sort of thing with tigers—but do not be too ambitious—you'll find your dog a lot easier to start with.

But now, in the next chapter, we must get back to the more serious side of training.

REFUSAL OF FOOD FROM STRANGERS

TEACHING a dog to refuse food from strangers is not only an obedience test carrying high marks, but it may save his life at some future date. The best burglar alarm ever invented is an alert dog, and attempts are sometimes made to poison the animal by means of food taken from the hand or dropped in his path.

One of the best methods of teaching refusal of food is taught in the absence of the owner. The services of a friend, not too well known to the dog, should be secured. A total stranger is even better, but few people will volunteer to tease a strange dog with food.

The trainer should flat the dog and bid him stay while he goes out of sight or away from the dog. The friend must then offer the dog a piece of meat and, in most cases, the dog will welcome this manna from heaven and reach forward to take it.

On no account must he be allowed to have it. The friend must snatch the meat away, grumble at the dog, and tap him sharply on the nose if he persists in trying to gain possession of the food. The words ' No! Don't touch! ' should be repeated emphatically.

Then offer the meat again and repeat. Reprimand and grumble at the dog at the slightest sign of acceptance and make it clear to him that he is not to accept whatever the temptation. Be very careful that he does not snatch it unexpectedly. Tempt him severely but never allow him to take the morsel in his mouth. After a while, if he is continually tempted and then baulked, he will lose interest and refuse to reach forward, turning his head away as the meat is offered.

Now is the time to try other tempting tactics. Throw the meat towards the dog—but be ready to pounce upon him with the correction if he tries to pick it up. Most dogs make an instinctive movement to catch a falling object and your assistant will have to move swiftly to prevent him seizing the morsel.

Dog being tempted
with food during an
obedience test

Try to make him take it by leaving a piece of food between his paws; leaving it near him on the ground, or patting him while he is tempted to take.

But be sure to snatch it away and scold him directly he tries to get it.

Make sure that your assistant is hard hearted! Most people feel like a cad when trying to tempt a dog to eat and then grumbling at him when he accepts. It may seem that the continual teasing will cause a dog to lose his faith in human nature. Curiously enough, it just teaches him to refuse food casually offered by a stranger.

This is probably because dogs think humans are crazy, anyway.

The owner can return and praise the dog after the lesson. It is essential to confine the praise to words and caresses. Do not, on any account, give him any sort of food as a reward, or the lesson will be entirely wasted.

The time will come when the animal will seem fool-proof and his owner will go around shooting a line about it. He'll challenge his friends to tempt the dog and very likely he'll get away with it for a time—until some fiend in human form produces a slice of fried chicken or a succulent leg of lamb — and away will go the owner's reputation as a trainer as the dog bolts the tasty morsel with all the zest of a politician kissing a voter's baby.

So do not rest content with the training until the dog has been tempted with all sorts of food—especially the ones for which he has a special weakness.

It is also possible to train with the owner standing near and forbidding him to touch as he attempts to take the food from the hand of an assistant. If the voice is not enough to deter him it must be accompanied by a rap on the nose from the owner and withdrawal of the food by the assistant. Dogs have been trained by both methods, but the former is usually more effective lest the dog come to depend upon his owner's presence as the deterrent and fall into temptation when he is absent.

Picking up food from the ground can be discouraged by spreading the bait and leading the dog into temptation. Pounce on him and scold severely when he is about to pick up. A strong deterrent is to bait a break-back mouse-trap with meat so that it jumps up into the dog's face when it is touched. The springs fitted to these traps are usually very strong and should be weakened very considerably before use. This is important because we do not wish to injure the animal but merely startle him and, perhaps, give his nose a mild rap. Remember—weaken the spring.

There is nothing at all unkind in either teaching refusal of food from the hand or from the ground. In the first case, dogs are often poisoned by ill-intentioned people, and in the second, animals are often tempted to pick up poisoned baits laid down for vermin.

Better a disappointed dog than a dead one.

CHAPTER 12

JUMPING

THERE are three types of jump which vary in height and length according to the breed of dog. We will take the high jump first.

It is possible to use obstacles such as a fence or wall, but training will be easier if a portable and adjustable unit can be constructed. The cost will vary with the availability of timber, but it is not necessary to buy expensive wood and the jump can be made very roughly from old timber. A coat of paint will work wonders in appearance.

Make two sides of stout section timber in the form of inverted T's, the horizontal portion resting upon the ground and of sufficient length to hold the supports steadily. The vertical length should be about five feet in height, but this can vary according to the size of the breed being trained.

Nail two strips of wood to form slots down each inside of the uprights so that boards may be slid between them and thus height built up as training proceeds. The boards should be about six inches in width.

As usual, training to jump is built up gradually. A dog will jump to please itself but it must be trained to jump upon command over a selected obstacle. Start with one six-inch section in place for a dog the size of a Corgi, and three

Dog jumping over the long
jump and through hoop.

Dog jumping through
hoop which gives him
only 1/8 inch clearance
all round.

sections for an animal like a German Shepherd. Be careful not to make it too high whatever the breed of dog—better start too low than too high.

Set up the jump and leash the dog. Retire a few feet for the run-up, and run with the dog towards the jump, taking care that the direction will enable you to pass on the outside although the dog will have to jump. As you reach the jump, command ' Over! ' very distinctly, and twitch the lead upwards. If all goes well, the animal will hop over easily and he can then be praised and jumped from the opposite direction.

Add another section to the jump and repeat, the dog still on the leash. Keep him jumping leashed for a few lessons and then run by his side with the dog running free, commanding ' Over! ' each time the jump is reached. Do not add too many sections too quickly. Keep the height well within the dog's capacity until he is jumping freely off leash and seems confident.

The next step is for the owner to leave the dog sitting and stand by the side of the jump. Call the dog and order him to go over. Put him on the leash again and take him over at the first sign of refusing or stalling, and then try him from the sit again. Repeat if necessary as many times as required. If he refuses consistently, lower the height a little and gradually increase as he becomes proficient.

It is now time to send him over while sitting at the trainer's side in front of the jump. Sit the dog and then gesture towards the jump, commanding ' Over! ' at the same time. Keep the height reasonably low for the first two attempts. If he refuses to go forward, you will have to take him over on the leash again. Another way is to throw something over the jump and urge the dog to go over after it. Most dogs, however, love jumping and quickly learn the command. Make a game of it and he will enjoy the lesson and regard it as play.

A time-honoured method of teaching a dog to jump is to confine him at the end of a narrow passage blocked by a gate or other obstacle at the opposite end. The trainer should stand behind this and call the dog, who will leap the obstacle in order to reach his owner. This is not such a good method as the animal is just overcoming an obstacle without thought and will walk round future obstacles which are not contained between walls.

It is well to teach the retrieve over an obstacle as soon as the dog has learnt to jump. This should not present much difficulty if he retrieves well already.

To do this, stand well up to the jump with the dog in the usual sitting position by your side. Throw the object over, wait, and tell the dog to fetch. He will usually go over all right, but, being an intelligent animal, will see no sense in jumping back when he can return so much more easily round the side.

Circumvent this by going close up to the jump directly he is over, and inciting him to return the same way. If he persists in coming round, drive him back again and insist that he returns over the jump. He should sit and present as usual when he returns. Do not blame him too much if he forgets the small details at first. He has had the jump added to the retrieve and it is your duty as a trainer to correct patiently any mistakes he makes and knit the various parts of the exercise together for him.

There is another form of high jump which is known as the scale. This cannot be cleared in a flying jump and the dog must leap as high as he can, get his front legs or paws over the top, and scramble his body over by digging his back toes into crevices in the boards. Alsatians, Dobermanns, Labradors and similar breeds can manage six feet quite well and some have been known to scale twelve feet and over. It is advisable to have an old mattress or sacks of straw at the jumping-down side if much of this is practised. In any case, it is very tiring for the dog and should not be overdone.

The scale is constructed in the same way as the high jump but the supports must be much heavier and more than six feet in height. It must remain steady while the dog is scrambling and it is only portable in the sense that a lorry will be needed to transport it. Crevices must be cut between the boards, or slats of wood nailed on, to give the dog a toe-hold.

Training is the same as for the high jump. Start low and increase the height gradually. The dog has already been taught to jump so it will not be necessary to start with the lowest board, but make the first jumps well within his capacity.

The first hitch will come when the height is just too great for

A German Shepherd Dog scrambling the scale.
The boards are slotted into the uprights and
may be adjusted to any height.

him to clear with a clean jump, and he may stall and refuse to take off. Try him again and excite and encourage him all you can. In all probability all will be well, but it may be necessary to get behind him and push him over if he hesitates continually. Once he has discovered it is possible, he will gain proficiency with practice. Always lower the height for a jump or two if he seems to hang fire at a certain height.

The dog must use a somewhat different technique for the scale. The high jump proper requires a lengthy run if it is to be jumped cleanly, whereas a more vertical leap is required in the scale. A much shorter run is needed for the initial leap, which must be high enough to enable the dog to either get his front legs over the top, or to secure toe-holds which will add to the impetus and so get the upper half of his body over the top. It is a mixture between a leap and a run up the boards of the jump and the dog will find this out for himself if he is allowed to take a long run and so exhaust himself trying to leap the jump clean. The scramble is a perfectly natural technique which any dog will adopt if he is faced with an obstacle. The difference is that our dog is doing it on command while the wild, or untrained, dog will only do it by necessity.

The long jump may be taught either before or after the high jump. A portable long jump can be constructed from boards about six inches in width by three-eighths in thickness. Sizes are approximate and may be altered to suit individual requirements.

Make the supports first and cut the first pair with the tops sloping at an angle of twenty degrees, and the height eighteen inches at the top of the slope. Cut a four-foot length of the board and screw on top. The first section is now ready.

Repeat with the following sections but cut the supports, sloping at the same angle, two inches lower than the section preceding it, and a little shorter. Five or six sections will be needed in all and they should nest into each other for portability. Paint white or some bright colour.

The jump is angled, and the heights different, so that the dog, with the tallest section at the end, can see the extent of the jump as he takes off.

Training technique is the same as for the high jump. Start with the sections close together and take him over on the lead. Do not forget the command ' Over ' as he reaches the jump.

Then widen the sections a little and take him over again. Try him unleashed as soon as you think he has the idea. Repeat on the leash if he fails. He must be jumping free before any great distance is reached because it is obviously physically impossible for a trainer to hold the leash of a dog while he is jumping much over three feet in length.

So, when the dog is jumping free, space the sections wider at each succeeding lesson. If he fails at a distance, shorten the jump and widen it again a little later. Do not try to make him jump too great a distance at first or he will come to dislike the exercise. Also, do not ask him to jump a distance which is beyond his powers. Constant failure reacts on dogs just as it does humans, and we all hate something at which we fail.

The total distance will vary with breeds. An Alsatian will clear anything from six feet to fifteen feet and over, but smaller dogs vary a lot. What would be easy for an active dog like a Corgi or a Sheltie would be impossible for a Dachshund.

A dog required to jump free should be left sitting at a distance while the trainer retires to the start of the long jump and then calls the dog. Never stand at the end of the jump and call the dog over. The reason for this is obvious—if the dog was required to jump a stream to retrieve something the other side he would probably refuse to jump if he was accustomed to see his owner at the end of the jump. Much the best way is to train the animal to jump from his owner's side.

Do not forget to give him practical work over streams, ditches and logs. A dog knows the difference between real work and training, so give him the opportunity to show you how clever he is . . . even if you have to invent the jobs!

There are a few ' do nots ' in jumping:

Do not keep it up too long. Jumping is very tiring.

Do not make the dog land on a hard surface too much— especially in the case of the scale. Put a mattress or straw at the landing side.

Do not teach a very young puppy to jump while its bones are soft and it is growing.

Do not ask a dog to jump anything beyond its physical capacity.

Scrambling the scale.
Always arrange for the
animal to land on soft
ground, straw or padded
bags

CHAPTER 13

TRACKING
ON AND OFF LEASH

TRACKING is one of the most useful accomplishments which a dog can possess and its uses are so obvious that no examples need be given. A whole book could be written on this absorbing subject, but the following instructions, if followed out carefully, will enable you to train your dog to become proficient in the art.

A dog does not necessarily follow the exact path of the tracklayer and, to understand just why this should be, we must consider scent and what it is.

Scent is generally understood to be the slightly oily exudation from all living bodies, human or animal. It is deposited in various ways. By footprints, the touch of garments or flesh upon walls, grass, or other objects, and the scent dropped and scattered from the body of the tracklayer.

It is volatile and windborne and evaporates quickly under a hot sun, but will remain effective for many hours under favourable conditions. It is borne away by running water and does not remain on still water except for an infinitesimal fraction of time. It is found on the ground and in the air. It is weaker on hard surfaces such as roads and pavements, and stronger on vegetation. Slightly damp grass gives the best scenting conditions.

A dog will often track by air scent when it is hot and strong. The scent will be hovering in the air and the animal will track with his nose up. It is a different story when the scent is weak. Then the tracker must lower his nose to the ground. If your dog appears to be running fast with his nose held high, he is not necessarily following a false line. He may be following an air scent.

Then again, the animal may track to either side of the actual line or waver from side to side. Scent is volatile and a cross wind blowing across the track will carry the scent away from the line and the dog will follow this until he eventually comes right in to the bearer of the scent, whether human or a dropped object. Wavering is due to air eddies and a changing wind distributing the scent unevenly.

In teaching a dog tracking, from the simple seek-back or seek-forward to the more elaborate track with its twists and turns extending over many miles, the trainer must constantly bear in mind that no human being has the faintest conception of the scenting powers of the dog. Not only can a dog detect odours impossible for a human to notice at all, but the animal must, and does, analyse scent.

Take an ordinary track over grass, for instance. The ground bears the natural scent of the soil, the vegetation growing upon it, tracks from other animals, human beings, and birds. There may be a host of other scents, all of which the dog has to disregard in favour of the particular scent which he has been ordered to follow. He must do this all the time he is tracking and in spite of new and different scents which will crop up as he covers the ground.

So be very sure that your dog is off the line before calling him off. If he is called off a correct line and, mistakenly, urged to seek again, he will be puzzled and upset and his tracking will suffer. It is much better, if in doubt, to leave it to the dog and follow his track to finality. If he proves wrong he should be given another track immediately, but do not be too severe in your correction lest the animal is discouraged. A good dog will like tracking, which is quite natural to him, and he should be encouraged rather than blamed after a mistake. Watch the dog carefully. If he is tracking with his nose to the ground and his tail high, leave him alone—he knows better than you and you have no means of putting your own nose to the ground and telling him that he is following the wrong scent.

Food is a useful adjunct to use in training and should be given as a reward at the end of the trail. Do not teach tracking after a heavy meal. The dog will be lethargic and indisposed to work. Some trainers give the dog his main meal of the day after a successful track but this, although good practice, is not always convenient, and a small tasty reward will serve instead.

Start training with your own scent and build up in gradual steps as in the seek-back. Flat the dog and walk away from him for about twenty yards in a straight line and drop an object at the end of the track before returning on the same line.

Top: Dog jumping through double hoops.

Bottom: A record long jump by Field Trials Champion William of Rockswall. These jumps can easily be constructed from rough wood

Call the dog to the stick marking the start of the track and give him the scent by pressing your hands over his nose, pointing to the ground and letting him sniff that, or by smelling an object belonging to you. In any case, vary the method of giving the scent from time to time as he progresses.

Tell the dog to seek and fetch. This should be easy as he has been taught to retrieve, to seek-back, and to discriminate scent. Moreover, he has seen your movements and knows where to go. If he does refuse, which is rather unlikely in a dog at this stage of obedience training, the trainer should walk to the object again, return, and urge the dog to go forward. After all, it is very little more than a simple retrieve at the short distance used at the first lesson and failure will most likely be due to faulty or hurried preliminary training or simple obstinacy on the part of the dog. Do not, however, take the dog to the object and show him. Use all the persuasion you can—even if you have to follow a pace after him continually using words of encouragement until he picks up. Praise him for this and let no words of blame escape your lips although, mentally, you may be calling him all the names in the calendar!

But we will assume that all goes well and that he returns the dummy. He will receive his due meed of praise and the next lesson will find him going a longer distance until, after a few lessons, you are leaving the dummy out of range of his eyesight. You will not have to go a long distance for this. A dog does not put implicit trust in his eyes but knows his nose cannot lie and he will instinctively put it to the ground, or in the air if the scent is strong, as soon as he realises that he cannot hunt by sight. Also, by this time he realises that he is being sent to track something down and return it to his owner. In the first few lessons it is useful to drag the feet through the grass in order to leave a strong scent and make it as easy for the dog as possible.

It is time to introduce turns when he is tracking a fair distance in a straight line. Again, do this gradually. Leave him, walk away about twenty yards and make a sharp-angled turn in either direction. Scrub the feet in the grass at the turn so as to leave a nice mat of scent, and drop the dummy a few yards beyond before returning on the same path to the dog and sending him.

This will not present many difficulties to the slow, careful tracker, but some dogs are more impetuous and rush off convinced that this is just another of those long-range retrieves. He will come to the turn and rush past it.

Do not shout at him. Wait and watch and you will see him check as he realises that the scent is no longer there. He will begin to cast around to pick it up. Leave him alone as he works and let him puzzle it out for himself. He will either succeed or become discouraged and give up. Encourage him with gentle, persuasive words. Walk up close to him if necessary and unobtrusively lead him to the object—lead is the wrong word because you should be behind the dog all the time. Let him think that he has found the object all by himself and then give him more and more practice. Shorten the distance of the track if necessary and then gradually lengthen.

The remainder of the training is just practice. Use longer tracks and more twists and turns. Build up gradually. Start the track with the animal out of sight and then put him on the line. Practise with him while on country walks by dropping an empty cigarette packet, glove, or any other object, and then sending him back for it. This is a long-range seek-back but it is tracking all the same. Call the dog off play and give him a track. Track over all sorts of surfaces and under all conditions —practice will make perfect.

The next step is to convert him to following a stranger's track, but be careful in your choice of an assistant. These are very often difficult to find because there is a certain amount of walking and waiting to be done. There are also the types who make it a personal contest between the dog and themselves and try to baffle the animal by all sorts of queer antics, twists and turns . . . just the sort of thing which the trainer does not want when he is trying to instil confidence in the dog during the first stages.

However, having found a suitable assistant, start gradually as usual. Let the tracklayer go off in full sight of the dog, return, give the scent by hand or on the ground, and the trainer can send him off. Encourage him if he hesitates. He will probably go all right but hesitate to pick up something bearing the strange scent. Encourage him by voice to pick up and return.

At this stage, it is advisable to allow the dog to take the

scent by sniffing the footsteps of the tracklayer, or smelling an
article left by him. Normally, a lost person or fugitive will not
be present to give a scent by hand, but this may be used for the
first lesson to give the dog confidence.

The rest of the training is the same as in training the dog to
track on your own scent. Build up distance and the twists and
turns gradually until he will track several miles. More than
one object can be left on the track, and it is a good idea to
allow the dog to find the tracklayer at the end of the trail.
Contrary to the opinion of those whose idea of a tracking dog
is built up on the pursuit of fugitive slaves as portrayed in
Uncle Tom's Cabin, it is not necessary for the dog to spring at
the tracklayer's throat or chase him up a tree! It will be quite
sufficient for him to finish the track successfully.

One word of warning. It is essential that the tracklayer
should keep out of sight. A tracklayer who continually pops
his head from behind a bush to shout ' Yo-ho! ' is a menace.
He attracts the dog's attention, distracts him from the ground
scent, and induces him to track by sight. The tracklayer must
stay hidden until found.

Do not always use the same tracklayer. Accustom the dog
to as many different scents as possible and do not always lay
the tracks over the same stretch of country.

But your tracking is not finished yet. So far, the dog has
tracked off a leash and it is now time to teach him to track
while under control. Leash tracking is used when it is necessary
for the handler to maintain close contact with his dog such as
in finding a lost child.

The equipment needed is a long, thin cord, as light as
possible, and varying in length from about twenty-five to fifty
feet. This is attached to a ring on the top of a harness passing
around the dog's chest and held in place by a yoke in front.

The trainer must be sure   to see that this does not drop
across his front legs and impede movement. He should be
accustomed to the feel of the harness before actual operations
are started. This can be done by dressing him up and sending
him back on a simple seek-back. He may hesitate as he feels
the slight pull of the cord through your fingers or against the
ground. He will soon become accustomed to the slight restraint but care must be taken not to jerk the cord in case he
takes this as a correction. In any case, it will disturb his

concentration. A steady pressure will ease him up if he goes too fast, but the less interference the better.

Leash tracking is just a variation of tracking free except that a strange tracklayer will have to be used from the start. Begin with simple tracks over a short distance to get the dog used to the leash, and work up to longer tracks with various twists and turns over varying terrain. Two or more objects may be dropped for the dog to find and it is always more satisfying to allow the dog to find the tracklayer at the end of the trail. This, however, is not strictly necessary at all times because there may be occasions when the dog will be used to recover stolen or lost objects only.

Two more variations may be introduced into tracking with or without leash. Time may be allowed to elapse before the dog is put on the line in order to allow the scent to grow cold. Again, do this gradually. There is no precise time during which a scent will remain useful. Claims have been made varying from the possible to the ridiculous but everything depends upon the weather, the ground, the number of people, animals, or traffic, passing over the track, and the nose of the individual dog. Some dogs will worry out an hours' old scent while others will not bother. However, as a general rule, if your dog will follow a three-hour-old scent, he can be considered a good tracker who will get the most out of a cold trail at any time.

The second variation is the cross trail. This is made by someone passing over the real track. Different cross tracks may be made by other tracklayers if it is desired to severely test the dog.

Let your commands be persuasive rather than forceful. Drawl out the word ' s-e-e-k,' for instance. Make no sudden movements or sudden twitches of the leash. Encouragement, not blame, should be the keynote in training the tracker. In any case, whatever the exercise being taught, there is no necessity to shout at the dog like a drill sergeant. After all, who loves a sergeant!

Above all, trust your dog until he is very obviously wrong. There will be times when he seems to be off the line and you will need all your patience to restrain yourself from taking a hand in the game. In most cases the dog will be proved right and the handler wrong. Tracklayers take a delight in saying

Close-up of simple,
home-made tracking
harness

that they will go one way and then making a turn in the opposite direction with the kindly intention of giving the dog more practice.

So remember that your dog is the only one who can pick up the scent and who has any check on the change of direction, so be very certain before you drag him off what you consider is a false line. If you are wrong, and the tracklayer emerges suddenly from a bush in front of you, you're going to look an awful fool.

And, very likely, the dog will turn round and ask who is training who!

CHAPTER 14

THE POLICE DOG

YOUR dog is now thoroughly trained in obedience and is becoming a useful tracker. Every succeeding lesson has made him more aware and easier to teach and he is a reliable companion who can be depended upon to behave himself under almost any circumstances.

At this stage the trainer may feel that the dog's education is complete and he may have no wish to go forward to the more specialised work of guarding and man-work.

There can be no quarrel with this very sensible attitude. It is not necessary for the family dog to be taught how to tackle a criminal and, in many cases, the animal will be too small to exert anything but a harrying movement, although he may be effective in giving the alarm and tracking.

There are, however, people who wish to enter competitions, need a guard dog for factories or for personal protection, and who would like to have some idea of the training involved. It is a complex business and only the main outline will be given in this chapter. It is well to remember that a dog badly trained to tackle a man can be as dangerous as a loaded automatic in the hands of a child. Generally speaking, it is better for the inexperienced trainer to leave police dogs to the Services or the real police.

Contrary to general opinion, it is not the dog with the

aggressive spirit and the tendency to bite which makes the best police dog. After all, a human policeman does not wander around the streets hitting all and sundry with his truncheon but reserves the use of force until it is necessary. So must it be with the dog. He must be friendly and inoffensive until he or his master are attacked or he is told to attack. More important still, he must cease to attack at the word to desist—and this obedience must be lightning fast. Any fool can teach a dog to bite—it takes good training to make a dog stop instantly or to give up the pursuit of a fleeing man.

So the dog must be fearless but with a good, even temperament, and he must not be excitable or dull. Above all, never teach a nervous dog man-work or you will have a nervous biter on your hands who will bring untold trouble to you sooner or later. It should be almost unnecessary to say that the dog must be well grounded in obedience and quick to obey every command.

Then a pseudo-criminal must be found. This is not easy because many people are afraid that they will be badly bitten. This is not the case and the criminal can even be a member of the trainer's own family and someone whom the dog knows well. The only equipment necessary is an old sack and, later on, a padded arm which can be slipped on for the dog to grip.

There is no attempt to make the dog attack viciously during the early stages of training. In any case, even with a real criminal, the dog is not intended to become a wild beast intent on a kill. If he is properly trained he will do an effective job without any personal hatred of the man he is arresting.

So find an empty sack, a criminal, and an object for the dog to guard, and we are all set for the first lesson.

Start with the dog tied to a post and ready to guard an object left with him. The trainer should be close by to praise or correct, but the real work must be left to the amateur criminal. It will rest with him to tease the dog so that he will bark a warning against the attempted robbery. The teasing must be carried out carefully because the intention is to give the animal the impression that this is a new and exciting game. Do not infuriate the dog and make him look upon the criminal as an enemy. The dog should be persuaded to strain after the man as in a game. This is just the opening stage and the dog

Criminal under escort.
The dog is ready to pursue
at any sign of escape.
Note the sacking padded arm

must not be given the impression that all strangers are hostile.

It is sometimes very difficult to make a dog bark just when we want—although we have all had the infuriating experience of trying to stop the noise upon all sorts of unnecessary occasions! One of the best methods is for the criminal to approach the dog and then suddenly turn and bolt back the other way. This will excite the pupil and generally bring a bark if it is repeated several times. The criminal can make weird and wonderful hissing sounds with his mouth and this will interest the dog greatly, very often bringing forth the desired bark.

A feint at the guarded object will achieve the same result, and there are many other devices which the trainer will be able to think up and suggest to his assistant.

It is the duty of the criminal to encourage the bark whenever it comes, and the dog should be enticed to give a full-throated chorus at any attempt to secure the guarded object. He will come to learn that a bark acts as a warning and it will keep him alert and watchful. It is the nature of a dog to bark at anything out of the normal, harmless or otherwise, and he is now barking with a definite object.

The next step is for the criminal to flick the empty sack at the dog as he turns away and try to make him bite it. A few lessons will soon teach him to seize the sack and hang on to it. He is encouraged in this by the criminal dancing about in front of him and running out of reach directly the dog relaxes his grip. By this time the dog is thoroughly enjoying the fun and goes for the sack every time it is offered.

But the criminal must not try to be too clever and try to grab the guarded object by crowding the dog into a corner. Neither must he become impatient if the animal does not bark enough or is slow in barking. It must be remembered that the dog is a friendly creature and it is not natural for him to attack a man viciously. He is being taught to do a job, and the criminal who crowds him in the early stages will baffle the dog and make him feel that he is being driven into a corner.

It is essential that the dog should continue to look upon the training as a game and it is usual for the budding police dog to jump all over his attacker with every sign of affection after the lesson is over.

This, then, is the first stage in the making of a police dog. He learns to bark a warning and grab a sack. The hardest part of the training is yet to come. He knows how to bite the sack and he must now be taught to let go. This must be done very thoroughly because the effectiveness of his early training will determine whether he is to make a loyal and dependable guard or become a potential danger.

It is important to realise at this stage that the initiative must always rest with the trainer and never with the dog. Command is important and the word to release can be anything so long as it is strong enough to cut into the dog's consciousness even during the excitement of the attack. Let it be sharp and short. Also, the trainer must be at hand so that he can reinforce the spoken word with action. Remember the order: Command first and action afterwards. Always in that order—this is important.

And let the action follow fast on the spoken word. Let the dog hold fast to the shaken sack, and then rip out the word to release, following immediately with some action such as rapping him on the nose to force him to obey. Remember, he does not yet recognise the word alone.

Dogs vary in their response and some will release at once, while others are more obstinate. The important thing is to accomplish the release in one smooth sequence of command followed by swift action. Never stand over the dog imploring him to release. He must be made to understand that this is one command in which hesitation will not be tolerated. The average trainer will, by this time, know the best action to use with his particular dog to enforce quick obedience.

The duty of the criminal is to stand perfectly still when he hears the command given to the dog. His stillness must synchronise with it because, later on, it will take the place of the command and the dog will stop his attack as soon as the criminal ceases to struggle.

Do not allow the dog to attack out of range of the trainer's voice and action too soon. Be very certain that the dog understands that he must cease to attack when the criminal ceases to fight. Test him again and again before he is allowed to attack where the handler's command cannot be followed by lightning action in the case of disobedience. This point is stressed and is supremely important. If the dog is allowed to

A police dog seizing the
padded arm at a
demonstration

get away with occasional disobedience at this stage he will never be dependable.

It is not easy to reach this perfection of training. Dogs are made of flesh and blood and have their vagaries. Some are easy to encourage and others just as easily discouraged. The actions of the criminal encourage him to bite, while the trainer's commands, followed by actions, discourage him. The attack and the breakaway should be mixed in the correct proportions to balance the dog. The sharp dog will be given plenty of orders to leave, while the dog shy of attack will be encouraged to do so.

However, the time will come when he can be trusted to try the arm grip on the sleeve worn by the criminal. It is well to give him the first lesson while on the leash. Reinforce the command to leave by a sharp jerk away on the leash when the criminal stops struggling. The pupil can then be walked round for a short way at heel to calm him down and get rid of any excess of excitement. The emphasis should be on the leave and not on the attack.

For the first lessons on the arm grip the criminal should leave an end free for the dog to grip and there should be no fear of a bite on any unprotected part of the body. The next step is for the sack to be wound tightly around the arm so that the dog must seize the entire arm in his mouth to get a grip. The hand should be protected with a stout, leather glove. The trainer should remain within easy reach so that he can follow his command by action should the dog forget and disobey the order to release, which is, in effect, the cessation of the struggle by the criminal. In any case, always stop the attack at the least sign of the animal becoming over-excited or showing signs of real pleasure in the biting part of the business.

Later on, the criminal may be armed with a cudgel or a gun. Try the cudgel first. The criminal should not lash out at the dog and try to injure him. The dog will be quite aware of the threatening potentialities of the stick and may hesitate to close in and attack. Here again, dogs differ. The bold will spring in regardless of the consequences, while others more cautious, and perhaps more intelligent, will content themselves by circling round the man and barking. In the former case the emphasis will be again on the release, while the cautious dog will be tempted to attack. It may be mentioned here that the cautious type is more likely to prove the best police dog in the long run. The ideal dog will dart in swiftly, immobilize the criminal by gripping his arm, and automatically release him when he ceases to struggle. It is most unlikely that any gunman will have retained a grip on his weapon more than a split second after a police dog has fastened his jaws around his arm.

A police dog should face firearms, but do not explode a pistol close to a dog's ear during the first lesson. Not only are a dog's ears far more sensitive than ours, but such a foolish procedure is almost certain to make him gun-shy for ever. Do it gradually, allow the dog to hear distant shots which are brought nearer and nearer. Let him attack the criminal holding the gun, but it should not be fired until the dog has lost his fear of the unknown. In any case, the criminal should first fire the pistol at the end of the field while the dog watches from a distance. This must be done again and again, coming nearer every time, until the dog no longer shows perturbation at the report and flash.

Here again, dogs vary a lot. Some seem to be naturally unafraid of guns, while great patience is required with others. Most of them will show uneasiness in various degrees at their first introduction to firearms. The Golden Rule, as in all training, is to take it by easy stages.

The next step is to teach quartering and baying when the criminal is found. On no account must the dog attack the man. He must be content with watching him and speaking the alarm.

This can be started by allowing the criminal to run to the shelter of a wire gate, the dog being released behind him. The criminal must make the dog bark by inciting him with movement and voice and the work should be improved each day until the dog can be restrained from attacking by means of a rope fastened to his collar by which he can be hauled back if necessary. The criminal, of course, will be in the open and not behind the gate.

When the dog is trained well enough to bark the alarm without attacking, the work may be carried out with the criminal at a distance and hidden behind some convenient object. Let the distance be fairly short for a start.

The trainer should wait until the criminal is hidden and then bring the dog into the field and command him by gesture to search the terrain by sections. The dog will find the hidden man in due course and, if all goes well, bark until his handler comes up.

Then follows escort work. There should be no difficulty about this, but any attempt by the dog to run in and seize the marching criminal should be strongly corrected. An occasional escape, in which the criminal breaks away and is pursued by the dog, may be given to keep him keen, but take care that this is not overdone.

In the same way, a dog left to guard a prisoner should not attack unless the man tries to escape—and the grip should be released at once when the man stops struggling. Again, this should not be practised too frequently.

Anyone who has attempted police-dog training will fully realize the supreme importance of an early grounding in obedience. This will become evident when the dog has to be recalled from his pursuit of a fugitive. The well-trained animal will return—the indifferently trained will continue his headlong career, and all the shouting, bellowing and imprecations in the world will not bring him back.

Training a police dog is not easy and no apology is made for repeating that it is best left alone unless there is a real need for a guard dog or the trainer is highly skilled in the art of training and control.

Remember, any fool can make a dog bite, and the accent in training should be on restraint and not attack.

Train slowly but very thoroughly.

CHAPTER 15

OBEDIENCE TESTS AND WORKING TRIALS

IT is possible that the dog owner who has followed the training schedule contained in this manual, and who now possesses a really well-trained dog, will be bitten by the training bug and wish to test his skill in competition with other trainers and their dogs.

Obedience tests and working trials are run at frequent intervals during the year by various canine societies in many towns spread all over the country. They are becoming increasingly popular at dog shows and the massed crowds around the obedience rings are a sure indication of the increasing interest in the working dog. These events are advertised regularly in the canine press and the secretary of any club will be pleased to supply schedules and particulars of the tests.

All dogs entered in Obedience Trials must be registered with The American Kennel Club, 221 Fourth Avenue, New York City. It is not necessary for a dog to possess a long line of illustrious ancestors, but he must be pure-bred. Castrated males and spayed females are eligible for competition.

There are hundreds of training clubs and classes throughout the United States and Canada. The majority are open to all breeds of dogs, but a few are limited to one special breed. Information may be obtained by writing to the American and Canadian Kennel Clubs or by making local inquiries. Some training classes operate independently, being sponsored by some civic organizations, while others, if they meet with all requirements, become member clubs of The American Kennel Club.

However, whatever your ambition, whether to make your companion an obedience champion or just a well-behaved citizen, by training him you have rendered a service to all dog lovers and shown that a dog is something more than a creature who delights in running under motor cars and spreading his loose hair all over the dining-room carpet.

You have shown the world that the ordinary dog in the home can become one of the world's workers and of service to his owner. Not for you will be the agonised shouting after the errant dog—but the quiet word of command, instantly obeyed by the animal, who is not only your dog but your friend.

Good Luck and Happy Training. . . .

INDEX

Entries that are completely capitalized indicate chapter headings.